T0326055

BRENDA BARRINGTON

A SMALL HOUSE IN France

How an English couple turned a neglected
French cottage, an acre of land and a walnut
orchard into a holiday retreat

BRENDA BARRINGTON

A SMALL HOUSE IN France

MEREO
Cirencester

Mereo Books

1A The Wool Market Dyer Street Cirencester Gloucestershire GL7 2PR
An imprint of Memoirs Publishing www.mereobooks.com

A Small House in France: 978-1-86151-154-6

First published in Great Britain in 2014
by Mereo Books, an imprint of Memoirs Publishing

Cover design - Ray Lipscombe

The address for Memoirs Publishing Group Limited can be found at
www.memoirspublishing.com

The Memoirs Publishing Group Ltd Reg. No. 7834348

The Memoirs Publishing Group supports both The Forest Stewardship Council® (FSC®)
and the PEFC® leading international forest-certification organisations. Our books
carrying both the FSC label and the PEFC® and are printed on FSC®-certified paper.
FSC® is the only forest-certification scheme supported by the leading environmental
organisations including Greenpeace. Our paper procurement policy can be found at
www.memoirspublishing.com/environment

Typeset in 10.5/16pt Plantin
by Wiltshire Associates Publisher Services Ltd. Printed and bound in Great Britain by
Printondemand-Worldwide, Peterborough PE2 6XD

To my Aunt Margie and her time at 'Le Petit Joyau'

Acknowledgements

Since we started our adventure many people have become interested in our project. Colleagues, friends and close family have witnessed our journeys to and from France and listened to our exploits. Our French neighbours are real individuals who we love dearly, but we have thought it prudent to change their names.

I hope Ray enjoys reading our story (which he has yet to do!) He is not a keen reader, spending so much time DIY-ing. It was only his determination that finished our project, along with his habit of perfecting everything he does. This often extends the work somewhat, but I forgive him.

Lastly, my sincere thanks to Chris Newton of Memoirs Books for his excellent editing. This, along with his patience and encouragement, enabled me to produce a greatly improved manuscript.

Contents

Introduction

Why have I decided to put pen to paper, or rather fingers to keyboard, to tell the story of the past decade? Let me explain. To most people the idea of approaching retirement is daunting. It means a big change of lifestyle. To some it is long awaited, to others it is viewed with some trepidation.

In my case I was lucky enough to have an ambitious plan on the horizon. Even more special, it was to be undertaken with Ray, my husband.

The seeds of the plan were sown eight years before our retirement. Our two children were at last becoming independent, if that ever happens! Our son had almost finished at university and our daughter was just beginning her three-year course. At last we could enjoy holidays that weren't designed to keep them amused.

So the first holiday by ourselves was to France. It was advertised by a holiday company as 'pay up front', with travel vouchers to be used at nominated hotels. You are free to select your own route. The journey began with the ferry to Brittany. Not finding good weather there, we headed south to find the sun.

Further and further we drove, until finally we found the sun shining at La Rochelle on the west coast. Next came the beautiful town of Royan. Stopping at more expensive hotels, we used two vouchers per night. By the end of our first week we were following a recommended wine trail leading to St Emilion near Bordeaux, and from there we ventured into the heart of the Dordogne. By now, with no vouchers left, we were completely lost to France and all her temptations.

Our return journey was through the Loire, back just in time to catch the ferry. We were already planning to explore in depth the wonderful places we had glimpsed on our whistle-stop tour.

The next three years we holidayed in France. On one of these holidays, having hired a small cruise boat along the pretty waterways around Redon in Brittany, we stopped to view some old, dilapidated cottages. My husband, now in his mid-fifties, was convinced he could restore a building like this to a habitable state, using his in-depth knowledge of 'do it yourself'. The plan was born.

On return from this holiday we decided to look further into the possibility of purchasing a property in France. We had three more years in full-time employment before taking retirement together at the age of sixty.

Since our marriage back in the 1960s we had gained valuable experience in renovating and extension work, thanks to numerous house moves. Both originating from London, we married young and moved to the West Country to start a new life where we could afford accommodation.

What if we could purchase a run-down building and use the early years of our retirement to restore it to our holiday home in France?

A dream takes shape

Enter a 'maison secondaire' in south-west France. Pass through the small lobby to a large room divided by a central staircase. On the right the dining area, bathed in sunlight from a tall window with external shutters, contains a large oval table surrounded by dining chairs; a pine dresser backs the ascending handrail of the stairway. In the corner a black wood-burning stove stands proud against a backdrop of antique red brickwork. A solid dark oak mantel supports wood panelling behind the flue pipe.

The supporting oak beams of the upper floor are exposed and outlined against white stippled plasterboard. Ornaments encircle the room, courtesy of the dark oak shelf, purpose-built to offset the ceiling height. Left of the staircase is the open-plan kitchen area. Solid pine units are fitted to the far wall, encasing kitchen appliances; another tall window reflects light onto the original floorboards, which have been stripped and varnished.

Take a seat in the armchair by the wood-burning stove and add a chunk of wood to the fire. It is late February, and bright blue skies are encouraging early spring flowers, but it is a touch chilly in the north-west wind. Enjoy an apéritif, a glass of Pineau des Charentes from the local region. The burning logs give off the sweet smell of applewood, along with plenty of warmth. Looking around the cosy surroundings, memories are roused of the preceding years. The room did not always look so inviting; indeed there was a time when the whole of the property was in a very sad state of neglect. The 'maison secondaire' adventure has yet to begin...

The idea of owning a property in France to become our second home appeared more realistic after attending the first French Property Exhibition held at Olympia, London. The venue had been well advertised in magazines and we decided a visit to this exhibition was essential to further our quest.

The literature, presented visually with graphic descriptions, offered buildings for sale in all regions of France at varying levels of habitation. There were crumbling stone walls under sagging roofs needing complete renovation; derelict farmhouses no longer occupied or required; old empty barns ripe for conversion, some with the added investment of a new roof to stop further deterioration. We saw complex parcels offering a large house with adjacent barn and outbuildings, remote skeletons of architecture by lakesides and many, many more as we turned the pages at the estate agents' stands. The sale price differed greatly according to the level at which the purchaser was prepared to take on restoration. Temptation was winning. What if we could transform one of these venues into a habitable residence during our impending retirement?

Our love affair with France had started eight years previously on a touring holiday, when we had realised just how greatly each region in France varied. Enjoying the excellent choice of accommodation, we would stay in *chambres d'hôte* (bed and breakfast in the owner's home) or the luxury surroundings of a venue selected from the book *Châteaux and Hotels of France*. During our travels we were able to sample the delicious cuisine from small cafés, bars, restaurants and large hotels. We continued to return each year on holiday, getting more captivated by France and all that was on offer.

Between our initial visit to the property exhibition and actually making a purchase, we made countless trips to explore individual villages in different regions. We needed to establish what we could get for the money we had to invest in the project. It took three years of visiting France twice a year to view areas we thought might prove suitable before we could make a decision. Arriving in a village picked out randomly on a map in England, you discover the disadvantages. It could look a perfect spot, close to easy travelling routes and handy to a large town to purchase renovation materials, but, as we perceived, every village is different.

In the countryside surrounding Toulouse nearly all the properties are in *bastide* towns, the unitary fortified towns built in the 13th and 14th centuries. The road leading towards the town gradually ascends upwards. In the medieval streets houses are built close together in solid ranks like defending soldiers. Here in narrow streets, a building signed *à vendre* (for sale) can be completely derelict. When peering in from behind the façade, there is no first floor or roof, just daylight between the walls of the adjoining houses. Indeed, these are restoration projects of gigantic proportions.

Bastide towns are steeped in history and fascinating to wander round, with their quaint roads and intricate passages. Solid wooden doors front each property, bearing scars of an age long past. You feel safe hidden in the depths of the stonework, like a fortress in history. We enjoyed visiting these lovely old towns but preferred to keep searching for a more rural aspect with the possibility of surrounding land.

Before each visit we would decide on new venues. After each village or town was explored it was crossed off our planned route, along with comments regarding suitability. Discovering that the region of Charente-Maritime boasted the most sunshine hours after the Mediterranean coast, we planned to extend our search along the coastline up from Bordeaux to the beautiful wine-growing areas around Cognac. Exploration revealed the properties to be of fairly large proportions and more expensive because of availability to the shoreline.

Our next trip was to be within the region of Deux-Sèvres. This area was recommended for unspoiled lakes and woodlands with plenty of sunshine hours yet still boasting realistic prices. The search was far from over yet.

Decision time

The Charente area and the medieval villages of the Dordogne were our favourite places in France. It was well advertised that finding a realistically-priced property for restoration in these areas was becoming more difficult due to their popularity with English, German and Dutch people wanting to purchase holiday homes. Articles in property magazines emphasized the advantages of extending the search for affordable homes to lesser-known villages in the regions of Deux-Sèvres or the Vienne.

On our next visit to France in February 2000 we had based ourselves just outside the small town of Civray, taking rented accommodation for one week. Before our trip we received literature from an English agent, a point of contact for a French estate agent (*un immobilier*) advertising a small cottage on the Charente-Dordogne border. Crossing to France from Portsmouth on the Friday night ferry, we travelled down to our accommodation during Saturday. As

Sunday was a free day we decided to check out the property. Monday would see us embarking on our tight schedule of pre-arranged appointments with immobiliers around Civray. It was a two-hour journey to this property, following the N10, then cutting across country to Chalais, the nearest town.

Using directions from the photocopied page of a map which had been attached to the house details, we eventually found it. The actual name of the village, Haut Bois, was not even marked on the 25:2 scale Michelin map which we normally use. The property was shown as *la maison dernière* in a *petit hameau* (hamlet) of a dozen assorted buildings scattered along a small, quiet road spread out over some five hundred metres from start to finish.

It was February, and the weather was very grey indeed. As I recall, the weather for the whole week was grey. But it can be to your advantage to see a property on a wet and windy day. Best you buy the property for itself and not for the sunshine.

We could see no 'for sale' sign anywhere on the property as we cautiously stepped out of the car onto a driveway consisting of nothing but two very muddy tracks. We knew it was the correct house as the picture in our possession matched the building. The lovely rural countryside on that dreary winter's day was very forlorn and lacked the sunshine to reflect the beauty and colour. The 'driveway' led round to the rear of the property, which was described as a "maison années 20 - hameau tranquille", ie an early twentieth century house in a quiet hamlet. It was built of concrete block, rendered and finished with a cream 'Tyrolean' coating which was now a dirty grey.

We observed two pairs of very tall shuttered windows at the front of the property and a very narrow front door to the north side. Outlining the shutters was white-painted stonework with red brick inserts arched over the top, which gave it some character. The roof looked in good repair and it boasted four chimneys, one in each corner. Sadly the south-west chimney stack had fallen to the ground, being a victim of the storms of December 27th 1999, violent winds that had done so much terrible damage to that region of France.

I remember putting on old trainers before tackling the very muddy ground surrounding the house. It was smaller than your average French country home, and very square in appearance. Round the back outbuildings joined the rear wall, appearing to form a useful workshop and storage area. There was only one entrance, the very faded paint-peeling front door. We walked round the property several times, studying it carefully; the strongest feature was the apparent solidness of its construction. Although the cottage was not built in natural stone as we would have preferred, the thickness of the walls showed that they were probably double skinned. Under the eaves thick solid wooden rafters, the roof supports, protruded at one-metre intervals along both sides of the building.

It intrigued us that this small cottage at the end of a hamlet was obviously empty and appeared totally neglected, from the external condition. A field and a white winding lane that disappeared into the distance separated it from the neighbouring property. The building had a further two tall windows with paint peeling shutters either side on the north and south walls. To the rear of the property was an acre of open field fringed with eight bare grey walnut trees which formed the eastern boundary.

The north side ran adjacent to the winding lane. The front faced west. To the south was a large grassed area with well-established shrubs and trees (one fallen). On the opposite side of the roadway, set well back behind gardens, was a large workshop alongside a very beautifully kept property with bright red shutters. This was the closest neighbour.

The other occupants of the hamlet lived in buildings of varying ages; two were clearly farmhouses with large yards, as there was evidence of tractors having gone to and fro leaving muddy tracks. We walked up the white lane, observing the deep ditches around the property, which contained fast running water, draining off the surrounding fields following the recent heavy rainfall.

The location was idyllic. The roadway we had arrived on merged into the distant landscape, which was devoid of any houses or habitation. The small house did look sadly neglected. It was obvious from the tightly-bolted shutters that it was not inhabited. We peered through a small letterbox to glimpse a very small lobby, and a musty smell drifted out. There was nothing else for us to view, so reluctantly we left, discussing what possibilities the house could hold inside.

As were leaving the sunshine suddenly appeared for a few moments from behind the grey clouds and briefly lit up the fields. We took this opportunity to take a few photographs. Good advice, given by another couple looking for property - take photographs and, if possible, use a camcorder. At the end of a busy viewing session it is easy to forget individual details. Memories of brief visits, especially when you are seeing so many buildings after long journeys, tend to fade quickly and you want to be absolutely sure of all the features when making your final decision.

Our accommodation for the week was a small rented cottage next to a large property owned by an English couple who had retired to France a few years previously and had completely refurbished their magnificent residence. No expense spared, it had been beautifully decorated in a French style with exposed beams and stonework. They showed us pictures of 'before' and 'after'. Their stonework had indeed been crumbling in parts. Seeing the finished results with the renovated cream stone masonry lovingly restored, along with a magnificent solid wood purpose-built French farmhouse style kitchen, made us feel very envious. This was a bit ambitious for us, not quite our intention, but certainly we had plans for exposed beams and stonework. They were interested to hear about our retirement plans and our search for a property.

Monday was spent viewing properties pre-arranged with a company we had met up with at the French Property Exhibition. We travelled quite a few miles that day, viewing at least six properties, with one standing out as a possibility.

Tuesday was spent with another immobilier who took us to a further four properties. Each had its own features and again one stood out amongst the others. Late on the Tuesday afternoon we contacted our Wednesday viewing agent, but were asked to swap to Thursday. This left us with Wednesday free.

We summarised what we had seen so far; a few very interesting properties which were far too large for us, and a charmingly-restored watermill alongside a stream, which was not too big, but some of the building was below floor level and the possibility of damp outweighed the good feelings we had for it. Others needed too much restoration, which would involve employing professionals, while some charming venues were already completed, which would defeat the objective of having a property to spend time and effort restoring.

So we agreed to use Wednesday to view the property we had seen on the Sunday, the last house in the *petit hameau* of Haut Bois. I rang the immobilier, keeping my fingers crossed that she would be able to meet us later in the day to show us the property.

"Yes you can come, it is not a problem" she said. She spoke very good English with a very heavy French accent. She would be more than happy to meet us at 12.30 pm to do a viewing. Out came the maps again, and we headed south on the N10 for a two-hour drive.

The estate agent's office was in the village of Aubeterre, only a fifteen-minute drive from the property. The village was one of historic beauty and displayed the sign "beaux villages des France". Villages with this sign mean they contain monuments of ancient history and beauty and have had investment by the French tourist industry to promote and encourage visitors.

The heart of the village was centred on a large square edged with trees. In the summer tables and chairs would be positioned under the shade from the nearby corner café and the square would fill with people laughing and chatting and enjoying the warmth. On Sunday mornings the square would be transformed into a *marché des légumes*, vegetable market, but on the day we first saw the square it was empty. The trees were bare of leaves and we sat in the corner café drinking a coffee and wondering what our reception would be like with our immobilière. Hopefully her English would be good enough to explain everything to us.

During our two previous years of searching for property we had both attended night classes for French conversation lessons. It was very slow going, but the over-riding incentive was the embarrassment we always felt when visiting France in not being able to converse with our French hosts. Most of the places we visited were rural and only French was spoken by the inhabitants. We had often practised our newly-acquired language, only to be greeted by blank expressions. After several attempts at the same sentence it was repeated back to us (always sounding the same as we had first said it). Then a long stream of French would follow which we could not understand, and we would feel totally deflated. Although, I would add, after each visit we did feel a little more confident, having managed to make ourselves marginally understood on rare occasions. There was no other choice but to press on with self-instruction of the language.

We entered the small office.

"Bonjour, bonjour, please come in, sit yourselves down, you are Monsieur and Madame Barrington?" I recognised the voice of the lady I had spoken to on the telephone. "My name is Marie-Claire and I will show you the property. Also we can see another one which is on the way, do you not think this a good idea?"

We agreed and marvelled at the speed she conducted everything. For some reason we took two cars, following her to the first property, which she seemed to think we would favour more than the one we had come to view. When we reached this property it turned out to be in Bonnes, a very pretty village by the river Dronne. The property was tucked away opposite a church dating back to the twelfth century.

After spending some time viewing this, Marie-Claire realised she did not have the key to open the cellar area. She used her mobile to contact the owner, who was leaving for Bordeaux within the hour. She explained that it was necessary to return to her office to meet him and get possession of the key. As time was tight we suggested we go onto the property we had come to see and she could join us after her trip back for the key. Marie-Claire agreed, although she was a little concerned, explaining that neighbours in the village might think we were trespassers. "I am sure it's OK as I will catch you up in a matter of minutes" she said.

Clutching the keys to 'the last house in the hamlet', we arrived at the property. This time the sun was shining, white fluffy clouds were being blown around and the weather seemed like an early spring day in England. We parked again on the driveway and ventured across to the front door. The sunlight lit up the surrounding area, showing up the small white lane winding off into the distance. With a backdrop of blue sky, the surrounding countryside looked alive and green instead of tired and grey as it had done on the last visit.

It was tricky to open the door; the key turned a few times but there appeared to be a knack in pulling the door a little before the last turn. Eventually we opened it and a rush of stale air greeted us. Just inside the front door was a very small lobby, only one metre square. A doorway on the left opened into a small room containing a shower, wash-basin and bidet. Directly opposite was a doorway to another small room. This contained a water heater fixed to the left-hand wall and a toilet with overhead cistern on the right.

We turned right through the lobby into a room which appeared to be the kitchen. A modern sink with a mixer tap was built into the corner of the room. The sink was housed in tired-looking wooden units which ran the length of the right-hand wall; on the top small mosaic tiles formed the worktop. We found the light switch and illuminated the room by a central bulb suspended on flex from the ceiling. Apart from the row of units the room was empty with two doors leading from it.

We turned left through the doorway into a second empty room. From this room yet another doorway led into the third room with a door leading back to the original room - the kitchen. We had walked a complete circle through four rooms. Each was approximately four metres square. How strange - all connected by doorways and completely empty. No exposed beams or stone walls. Very disappointing.

Then we noticed the floor; solid floorboards throughout. We thought the house smelt musty, but it did not feel damp. Although it was February it felt quite warm inside, although there was no heating anywhere as no one was living there.

At this stage of exploration Marie-Claire turned up. "Hello, hello I am here. It is so dark in here, n'est-ce pas? I will open the shutters."

Each of the four rooms had a window which, after pushing back the tall shutters, Marie-Claire flung open to reveal daylight. It was amazing. Suddenly the small house filled with light and you could see the surrounding countryside from every window. With each room being three metres in height, it felt quite spacious. Every window area was exactly the same size, a metre wide by two metres in height. They were opened by a central bar through the handle. Apart from being devoid of paint, down to bare wood in places with most of the putty missing outside, they could be saved with a lot of work to stop further deterioration.

Marie-Claire showed us a trapdoor in the wooden floor, which she opened. It revealed how high the floorboards were above the earth below. She wanted to emphasize to us that the ground under the cottage was not bare earth but hardcore. This explained why the house did not feel damp; it was built high above the soil, with solid foundations for the external walls.

We asked if the loft area could be used for extra accommodation. Unfortunately the only entrance into the loft was through a small metre-square external wooden door positioned over the roof of the workshop at the rear of the property; a ladder was needed to climb over the tiles to reach the tiny doorway.

We observed small fireplaces in three of the rooms, built on an angle into the far corner of each outside wall. We asked about the chimney, which had fallen down outside in the garden and was lying alongside the house.

"You do not have to worry about that" she said. "It will be rebuilt before the new owners move in. It is storm damage from the terrible recent tempest and the builders are working non-stop. There are waiting lists for the urgent work first, but it is not a problem and will be repaired before the sale." She said all this very quickly in her lovely French accent. "Have you seen enough? I will take you outside".

Actually there was nothing left to see inside, as all the rooms were completely empty. We followed her round to the back of the property. She pointed out there was a *puits* (well), and we dropped a stone down it. A long wait then a splash – yes, definitely a well with water at the bottom.

As she opened a door to the outbuilding it revealed a very large four-metre square dry workshop with power and lights; perfect for a person embarking on a large DIY project. Next to this was another locked heavy door; this too was opened and we peered into the darkness. It contained old sinks and rubbish, but could prove a useful lockable storage area.

"It is a very small house and it has been used by tenants who had not been kind to it" she said. "The owners have now decided to sell it. Although it needs a lot of decoration it has water and electricity so it is habitable, is it not?"

We agreed, and emphasised to her that we did only require a small house. Marie-Claire explained that she had another urgent appointment, so we decided we would all return to her office in the village centre. In the office we were given a set of up-to-date particulars of both properties. She said she would ask the owners about the state of the *le grenier* (loft) so she could tell us whether it could be turned into further accommodation.

At this stage we explained that we were staying outside the area and were viewing houses by appointment the next day. We said we would seriously consider this property, along with all the others. We had two more days of viewing. We said our farewells and promised to be in contact by telephone.

We decided to visit the café in the square again for some refreshments, and only then did we see what a quaint place it was. The café and restaurant were on the ground floor, while the next level was also a restaurant laid up with white tablecloths; above this restaurant were another three floors. Then we realised it was actually a hotel. The undulating levels of the square provided an entrance round the side directly to the first floor. From this entrance you passed the kitchen to the left and opposite the restaurant with the white tablecloths laid up ready for evening meals.

Inside the café two smartly-dressed waitresses expertly negotiated the staircase to the kitchen, fetching down appetizing lunches to customers preferring to eat in the café area. Behind a well-stocked, brightly-lit corner bar which backed onto the staircase, a short portly Frenchman, with a receding hairline, kept taking a puff from a cigarette in an ashtray hidden behind the counter while calling out to the staff. It could almost have been a scene out of the television sitcom *'Allo 'Allo*.

The wooden tables and chairs were rustic; there was a very uneven, but magnificent, dark solid oak staircase which turned on every step, inviting you up to the next level. Interesting pictures by French artists decorated the plain smoke-yellowed walls, while framed black-and-white photographs of the village depicted life in the past century. Customers stood around the bar engrossed in deep conversation, acknowledging each newcomer with an embrace of handshakes and kisses. The atmosphere was so very French. We ordered a sandwich and wine and savoured the ambience.

Next day we continued with more house-hunting, encountering another remarkable agent who took us to eight properties. We set off sharp at 9 am and were finished by lunchtime. Although we did manage to snap some photos we were given full particulars of each property. Overall we were shown some very interesting buildings. We returned to our cottage exhausted and spent the rest of the afternoon discussing what we had seen. We analysed each one for its merit and possibility for our retirement project. A lot of the properties which had solid stone walls felt cold on entering, especially if they had been left vacant. Also solid concrete floors did not help the warmth factor. A few homes boasted a white stone fireplace as a central feature along with splendid solid oak beams and inside walls of natural stonework - so full of character – but, unfortunately for us, too large.

During conversations that morning our immobilière had recommended a restaurant in a nearby town. We decided to visit and enjoy the cuisine on offer. True to her recommendation it was an excellent meal. We dined alone, apart from one couple who came and left before we had finished. After all, it was February and a damp and cold evening. We chatted about the properties viewed that week, going over the good and bad features. We loved the location of the small house at the end of Haut Bois in the 'hameau tranquille', but it did not have the essential criteria - natural stone walls and exposed beams. We finally decided it was not for us.

Friday morning we woke up to an awfully wet day. This was the last day for our pre-arranged appointments. We had visited a different estate agent each day, having finalised details with them prior to leaving England. We went to see the last agent on our list. The two properties we had been promised for viewing had been sold; again we were taken to one that was far too large. It would have looked fantastic when finished, but the restoration materials would be costly and professional work a necessity.

We returned to our accommodation at midday. So that was it; during the week we had actually visited twenty-three properties and thoroughly considered each one on its own merit. None had seemed to be the right one. What were we doing here in this awful weather anyway? We consoled ourselves that we had just picked a wet week.

The plan for our retirement, only three years away, was to visit France during the winter months of February, March and April and enjoy warmer, sunnier and drier weather than England offered. It was quite important to us to have a cottage that would feel inviting and not too large to be heated economically. Ray wanted to use the cottage as a project for his DIY skills. Once the basic work of turning it into a comfortable home was finished, we could use the accommodation as a base to travel to other destinations. France has a good rail network, with very fast modern high-speed trains and realistically-priced tickets, making it affordable to reach many places. We planned to return during the months of September and October and enjoy the warm French autumns. These were the basic criteria for our retirement plans.

After lunch it was still raining, not even a chance of a walk. Ray said he felt tired and would take a short sleep. I felt quite depressed at this point. We had come very close to making a decision on the little property on the Charente-Dordogne border, but because it did not have stone walls and exposed beams we had rejected it. It lacked the character of old exterior stonework, uneven internal walls and ancient beamed ceilings. It was after all quite modern, having been built around 1930.

I sat thinking about the small cottage. I felt that despite its drawbacks, it could be the right one for us. It certainly had a lot going for it, especially with the lovely countryside location. It was small enough to manage and felt warm inside. There was no major reconstruction work, which would have been inevitable on a lot of the other properties we had viewed. The construction was very sound and solid and I felt it had a lot of character – well, potential character; it just needed finding, bringing out, discovering - was that not the object of restoration?

Ray would undertake most of the work himself, having been an electrician in his early working life. Plumbing was not a problem, as he had already installed a bathroom at our existing house. Plastering walls was definitely a 'no-go' however, as we had abandoned a previous effort and called out a professional plasterer. His carpentry skills were fairly basic but he had received good groundwork in this area from my late father, a carpenter by trade, assisting Dad in building us a workshop and many other projects involving woodwork. He owned many modern electric tools and had inherited a lifetime's carpentry instruments from my father, so I had complete faith that Ray was more than competent to undertake the basic restoration work required.

I started to sketch up plans for the layout of the four rooms. We had discussed the possibility of a staircase being added, extending the accommodation into the loft. This would allow the installation of a fair-sized bathroom and a master bedroom. The downstairs would then be freed up for living accommodation. Two of the rooms could be made into one open-plan area, where the staircase would be sited.

I was now getting quite emotional about the situation and an inner voice seemed to be taking over. We were due to return home tomorrow with a long drive ahead of us, and it would appear we had lost our chance.

I felt deeply attracted to this property and by rejecting it I knew I would be haunted by regret for a long time. Of course, we might come upon the perfect property in a future house-hunting quest, but as each month passed before our next return visit to France, property values would keep increasing. It was now three years since our initial visit to the French Property Exhibition, and we knew through the monthly property magazines that prices had definitely been escalating, especially during the last six months. The money to finance the purchase of the cottage was from the maturing of two five-year savings accounts. This sum was enough to cover the majority of the purchase. The restoration money would depend on the extent of work necessary and that would be from our savings. We had no intention of taking out a mortgage; coming up to early retirement, our funds would be limited.

Ray, refreshed from his nap, joined me for a cup of tea. I decided to tell him my strong feelings for the small cottage and how it could meet so many of our expectations, offering sketches showing an added staircase and a new layout of the rooms. I asked him to seriously consider what we were turning down. There was so much going for the small house. The time was now four o'clock.

In-depth discussions continued for another hour. Practical and logical reasons were put forward. So much depended on whether we could make use of the loft area. Would it lend itself to being opened up and windows put in? Without having been able to view the area, we could not possibly know the answer, and would be taking a risk.

We finally decided to go for it. I was one hundred percent decided, but I guess Ray was still only ninety-five percent.

At five o'clock I phoned the immobilière. If she had left for the day it would definitely have to be a 'no go'. She answered, and I explained that we would like to make an offer on the understanding that we would be prepared to sign before we returned to England tomorrow. Marie-Claire explained that she would telephone the owners and ring me back. Apparently the vendors were an older couple; the husband was away but the wife would ring him to see if he was agreeable to our offer.

I started preparing and cooking a meal and Ray went up to start packing the cases. We were almost through eating our meal and were resigned to the idea that the estate agent had not been successful. Anyway, if she had been lucky enough to contact the owners they were bound to reject the first offer. I was prepared to up the offer with the immobilière should she ring back with a deadline price. But hope was fading. Surely business had closed now until the next day, and for us the next day would be too late.

Then the phone rang - it was Marie-Claire.

"It is good news for you. Your offer has been accepted" she said. "The owners agree to your price if you are prepared to sign the papers before you return to England. I will meet you in my office tomorrow, Saturday. Will 9.30 am be all right? We will do the signing. No problem. I will get all the papers necessary to commence the purchase."

I could not really believe it, talk about eleventh hour! It would seem we might be returning home with a *maison secondaire* after all.

We finished our meal in a state of shock and excitement. We felt like celebrating, but then remembered we had previously arranged to have a farewell drink on the last night of our stay with the English couple who had rented us the cottage. No time to dally, but we did finish up the open bottle of wine, toasting ourselves on our good fortune. We rushed on with the packing, as it would mean a very early start at half-seven the following morning.

Our hosts were very pleased to hear our news and that we had been rewarded at the end of our exhausting week. We explained that we would be setting off very early the next morning and gave them our thanks for all their kind advice during the week and the enjoyable stay in their cosy little annexe cottage. We promised to let them know the outcome and if the purchase was successful.

The next morning we slipped out, closing the large wrought iron gates behind us. We knew the best route, as we had done the journey twice before. It took us two hours and we arrived as planned at 9.30. We started making plans on the journey for our return to start the renovations. If we were lucky and the sale went through within three months, we could return in May.

To make the property more habitable, the first jobs would be a new toilet and the installation of a bath. If we intended to do this in May we would need critical measurements; did we have time to squeeze in another visit to the cottage? We had to be back that night for the ferry crossing at 22.00 and right now we were driving in the opposite direction. It was going to be a long day.

It was really quite amazing; everything was calmly conducted by Marie-Claire in about an hour. Initially we had to sign a contract to say we would purchase this property and pay ten percent of the agreed price. It was legally binding once our deposit had been forwarded over to France. The deposit would be forfeited if we did not go further with the purchase. She had prepared the necessary forms for signature before our arrival and explained, in great length, how best for us to get the deposit to the *le notaire* (solicitor), who would handle the sale on behalf of both parties. She gave us particulars of a local bank to enable us to open a French bank account and even came up with an insurance agent in Bordeaux who could offer us a quotation in English to insure the building after exchanging contracts.

We asked if we could have the keys again to visit the property and take measurements, promising to return them before one o'clock. Marie-Claire explained that she was shutting up the office and going off to enjoy the weekend, so we assured her we would be back by then. It was 10.30 and our first stop was the nearest village, Saint Aulaye, to find the bread shop - most important.

It was a great village containing a mini-market called "Huit-a-Huit" (open eight to eight) along with four butchers, three hairdressers and two bread shops. There was a large *hotel de ville* (town hall) and a local hospital, more like a small town than a village. This village was not where our local mayor (*le Maire*) was situated. Our *Mairie* (local mayor's office) was in another village which we did not have time to visit. Having satisfied ourselves we could get our bread with only a seven-minute car drive (we were later to find out we could cycle there on country lanes in twenty minutes, if we felt energetic) we returned to the cottage.

We only had an hour to take the vital measurements for our plans. We established that the dividing wall between the two very small rooms forming the washing and toilet facilities could be demolished. All the sanitary ware would be ripped out and replaced with a full sized bath, small wash-basin and new low-flush toilet. The water-heater would have to be re-sited on the right-hand side of the room, as the wall it was on at present would be demolished. The new larger bathroom planned for the first-floor was light years away; our initial thoughts on the first visit were to make the toilet facilities habitable. The existing amenities were far too ancient to put up with for any length of time. Also a full-sized bath was absolutely essential as far as priorities go.

There was no way, without a ladder, that we could get into the loft area, which was a great pity. This was a very large question mark in our plans. We took photographs and video footage of the inside to show the family. Soon our time was up and we had to leave in order to keep our promise and hand back the keys.

It was now 12.30 pm. We visited the corner café in the square for some light lunch before setting off on the long journey to the ferryport. A young French couple were sitting opposite us on the large corner table, having just merrily enjoyed lunch with friends. They pushed across a wine bottle containing the remains of some rosé, indicating to us to join them in a drink. We reluctantly declined because of driving. With difficulty we tried to explain that we had a long car journey and needed all our wits about us to make sure we caught the ferry which was leaving at 22.00 from St Malo. I doubt if they understood our French explanation for our refusal. We could have quite happily continued to sit in that pleasant café enjoying the quiet babble of conversation and indulging in the local *vin de pays*, but we had to make urgent tracks.

We arrived at the ferryport in good time, thanks to good driving conditions and well signed autoroutes. On board I telephoned our son and daughter with the news, unable to contain my excitement at the thought of returning to our own property in France in the future. They were both surprised to hear our news. They had probably thought it was only a bit of a dream and wishful thinking on our part and that it was never going to become a reality.

A strange incident occurred the next morning. The ferry was due to dock early in Portsmouth, so we were sharp into the restaurant for breakfast. Ray then spotted someone he knew. "That's Brian over there, Brian from the French night classes" he said.

I recognised our colleague. He was with his wife, who had not attended classes because she already had a good basic knowledge of French. Brian was very surprised to see us and introduced us to Judy. We knew they had purchased a cottage in France approximately eighteen months previously. Brian had shown us photographs and explained his future plans for alterations and improvements. We had often chatted with him at classes as he had known of our plans to find a property in France.

They were returning from a visit to their cottage because of damage done to the roof during the recent December storms and had found that ten trees on their land had been brought down. Arrangements had been put in hand for urgent repairs to the roof and to get the trees moved and logged up in early spring by a local contractor.

We explained that we had just signed to buy a small property and described the situation and location. It turned out that it was less than fifteen kilometres from their French home, only half an hour's drive. It seemed unbelievable that we could have purchased properties so close to each other when France is such a large country.

"When do you hope to complete?" asked Brian.

"In early May, if everything goes through smoothly" I replied. We told them our plans were to return during that month to get started on making it habitable.

"That's a coincidence, we're going back to our cottage in May" said Judy. "You must come over to see it and we'll spend the day showing you round our area. The most important place is the local *bricolage* to get all the DIY materials and you definitely need to know the whereabouts of the local *déchetterie*, the rubbish recycling centre."

At that time I did not fully understand the importance placed on the rubbish depot. Now I do. France is very strict about disposing of rubbish and the déchetterie is an essential address to have on your list of contacts.

We swapped home telephone numbers to keep in touch for the forthcoming arrangements. This was certainly going to be a great bonus for us, not only having the benefit of friends in the area where we were going with local knowledge, but newly-found neighbours in England with whom we were to form a close relationship with over the coming years. They lived less than a mile away from us. Small world indeed, or was fate playing a part in this?

We had finished with the evening classes some nine months previously, and did not intend rejoining. Had we not bumped into Brian and Judy that morning on the ferry we could easily be going to and fro from France without ever knowing of their similar circumstances.

In at the deep end

On our return to England we were on a tremendous high for the next few weeks. As we completed all the necessary paperwork, we kept in constant liaison with our French *immobilière*. Her help and assistance were invaluable; there was full determination on our part to keep the transaction rolling for completion in early May 2000. In France searches had to be confirmed on the land that was attached to the property, and knowing how slow legal matters can take in France, I was amazed that everything fell into place and we were able to make plans to travel over for completion on 4th May.

Although in our late fifties and still in full-time employment, we were in good health and felt confident to take on such a project. Ray was an avid 'do it yourselfer' following many house moves into properties which had required improvements.

We had met when I was seventeen and attending a secretarial college. On Saturdays I worked in the food hall at a large departmental store, where Ray was working in Boots and Shoes. The store was rambling and very old fashioned, something on the lines of the television comedy *Are You Being Served?* One day I had been told to fetch a fire bucket from another area, though why I can't possibly remember. My journey happened to be through Menswear, where Ray had been promoted for a month. This is where I encountered him, a handsome young man combing his Tony Curtis haircut. "Where's the fire?" he called to me. I laughed and went on my way. Afterwards he said it was the white uniform with the head-band clipped into my hair that he fancied.

Being very young we then embarked on quite a long courtship. Living in London in the early sixties there was no way we could afford any sort of property. Even the most basic and run-down was way out of our league. After our wedding at the ripe age of twenty-one and Ray twenty-two, we set off west to seek our fortune. We could just about afford a mortgage on a new small semi-bungalow (half the price of anything in London) in the remote little town of Melksham, Wiltshire. Since his menswear days Ray had managed several career moves. In London aged nineteen he was eventually taken on as an electrician's mate, being too old to undertake a proper apprenticeship. Having wired wall lights and a cooker plug for his mother, by way of written instructions from an electrician, he found a natural flair and an attraction to this trade. The electrician had inspected his work and was impressed, getting him an interview with the Southern Electricity Board (as it was called in those days).

On moving to Melksham he applied for a transfer within

the SEB to work in Wiltshire. They did not employ 'mates', but on interviewing him found he had worked on MICC (mineral insulated copper conductors) in London, so he was successfully transferred and promoted to full electrician status. They needed a person with this knowledge to wire a country church. So from London to the rural life; his first job involved swaying thirty feet up a ladder in the freezing cold winter, wiring a church in the remote village of Keevil.

We found Melksham very quiet after London, but after a year we liked it enough not to want to return to our roots. Because of career moves we went to various properties around the outskirts of Bristol. It was there Ray was able to attend night school to gain a City & Guilds certificate that would give him his paper qualifications as an electrician. Then on leaving the industry he took a short trial in salesmanship (definitely not his area). This led to him starting a new trade as a television engineer, again taking several years to qualify. Diversification was his strength really; he was always happiest when he could be involved with a new challenge on some project or other and was never afraid to tackle something new.

But back to the present: our new adventure in France. The cottage could be classed as basically habitable as it had the two essential services, water and electricity. We planned to take two weeks' holiday immediately after completion to get the property into a tidy state. May 11th was going to be the date for setting off to our new adventure. The full restoration project would take place in retirement with us spending the spring and autumn months over in France, where we would, hopefully, enjoy a sunnier climate, away from the inconsistent weather patterns of England. We had three more years before this plan could be put into practice.

Meanwhile we intended to use our annual holiday leave to make a start. The alternative would be to wait for retirement, which would not have been a good move as further deterioration was inevitable. It might have meant less stress trying to tackle a run-down property on a two-week holiday visit, but because we were taking over the existing electricity and water accounts, we might as well profit by using the property for a base in France. By having a working holiday we could combine any free time to explore the region.

The decision to acquire a trailer for our first trip was a priority, the logic being that on future visits the trailer would hold materials for the restoration and more furnishings for the cottage. Ray found a small company in Dorset making very sturdy trailers. Investing in a strong, wooden design with a ladder extension, we found it to be one of the most invaluable items we ever purchased. The size agreed was 6ft x 4ft, based on the advice of the manufacturer. Our strategy was to place heavy items over the floor area up to the height of the sides, concentrating them to the front and over the axle. Then across the trailer sides you lay four strong wooden slats and secure these to the side edges. Large items could then be placed on these supports. For example it could easily accommodate a double bed, which would only overlap the sides by a few inches. This would provide a solid base to support other items, gradually building up to the height of the ladder rack. Then you cover the whole load with plastic sheeting and rope down securely, pulling straps through the cleats strategically placed around the trailer. This method was followed for each trip.

Using the measurements of the two small sanitary rooms taken during our visit to the cottage, Ray drew a scale plan showing the dividing wall removed. In the remaining "L" shaped area he allocated space for a full-length bath, wash-basin and low-level toilet. On the fourth attempt there was a glimmer of hope that all three items would fit. A white bath was purchased from a large local store at half price. Ray knew French copper pipe and plumbing connections were metric and differed from the English fittings, so it was not practical to take these. The newly-installed toilet and wash-basin would be connected to the existing French pipework using the French plumbing materials, so all accessories would be purchased in France.

The bathroom installation would be the project for the initial two-week stay, then a general tidy up of the cottage, adding a few furnishings to make it homely. A list of the tools required for our first visit was started, adding essential basic materials. It was amazing how many tools were required; I just thought we would take an electric drill and a few other items. Unfortunately, that was not the case! Ray explained he needed all his plumbing kit, along with a full set of electrician's tools, woodworking tools including saws, chisels, hammers, grips, clamps and various sets of spanners. The 'do-it-yourselfer' in his own home just goes to his workshop or garage for the necessary equipment; working away from home, all these tools would have to accompany us and then return home afterwards.

A secretarial career had served me well throughout my working life and I had always easily found employment. I worked part-time after our children were born for several years before returning to full-time positions. I was now Personal Assistant to the Managing Director of an information technology systems company in Chippenham, where I commuted each day from Bristol.

One of my lifetime hobbies involved needlework, and designing and making clothes had been my first love. Using my knowledge of materials I diversified into making colourful cushions, curtains and eventually upholstery. This would be very useful for the home furnishings at the cottage.

As the cottage was completely empty there had been no option of purchasing furniture from the former owners. Essential items were needed to make a start the moment we arrived; basics such as buckets, bowls, brooms etc. Next on the list was something to sit on, possibly two comfortable armchairs if we had the space. I decided on a flatpack for a small round table along with four chairs for assembly on arrival. A double bed was on the list, along with bedding and curtains for a couple of the rooms. We decided that we would purchase a cooker and fridge locally. Basic crockery, cutlery and cooking utensils had to be added to the never-ending list.

The actual completion, signing and handing over of the keys was going to be a week before our two-week visit. For this we decided to travel over by air and train; it was quicker and less tiring than driving down and back within the space of three days. The route was via the TGV (*Train à Grande Vitesse*), France's high-speed train. We would catch an aeroplane from Bristol Airport to Charles de Gaulle Airport just outside Paris, and then make a connection to the fast train. This would take us to Angoulême. From here we could travel on the SNCF train along the regional line which would stop at Chalais, the local station, then by taxi for the last stage of the journey. Because we had to be at the estates agent's office early on the morning of the 4th May our train connections required us to spend a night in one of the hotels close to Angoulême station.

The money for the cottage had been transferred over into an account held by the notaire in readiness for the actual day of purchase. Our new French bank account had been opened and we had received a French cheque book, which seemed quite challenging. Resorting to my French books, I started some revision to familiarise myself with French numbers in readiness for mastering the cheque book.

As the date drew closer Marie-Claire confirmed that everything was on for the 4th May, so I went ahead and ordered the tickets for the impending visit. We were so excited; it did not seem real that it was going ahead at last. After months of discussion and planning, now finally we could get started. There was apprehension as to what we could expect on this new venture, but our thoughts were mostly occupied in ensuring the cottage was successfully signed over. We hoped it would all go through smoothly, with no last-minute problems.

May 4th at last, and the journey over to France went very smoothly with all the necessary connections. After spending the night at the hotel in Angoulême we strolled across the road to the station, where the regional train arrived, punctual to the minute. We sat back on the last part of the journey; the countryside rolled by outside and it began to look more and more interesting with undulating hillsides and brightly-coloured crop fields. We pulled into Chalais station and alighted from the air-conditioned train, noticing the heat. Jackets came off as we walked along the platform in the sunshine; we were the only people leaving the train.

Next we had to find a taxi. The station yard was deserted, so we walked the short distance into the high street. Still not seeing any taxis, we enquired in the local newsagents. My French sounded very basic as I ventured "Je voudrais un taxi, s'il vous plaît".

The assistant looked puzzled and then eventually got the *jaune annuaire* (yellow pages) from behind the counter. He looked up a number and wrote it down for me.

I used the mobile and then the fun started. I gathered the driver could take us to the destination, but I could not work out where the driver was. She kept repeating the words, "Intermarché - je suis en face du supermarché". Oh god, what now?

We walked across the road and down a narrow slope which opened into an area with a supermarket and filling station; we then spotted a taxi outside the supermarket. Yes that was her, we were OK.

The taxi pulled into the square where the estate agent's office was situated. We arranged with the driver that she would collect us at 14.30 for our return train to Angoulême. The square was alive with people. The trees, which had been bare in February, were now offering shade over the seating and the warm sunshine was dappling through the branches. We sat on a bench in the square, absorbing all the scenery and hoped everything would go to plan.

On arrival at the estate agents we were greeted with kisses and handshakes as though we were old friends. "Your journey was good, was it not?" said Marie-Claire.
"The vendors Monsieur and Madame Vallade will arrive shortly, then we will walk up to the notaire's office and do the completion".

We were introduced to the vendors, who again greeted us with handshakes and burst of welcoming French, to which we could only reply "bonjour". Together we all strolled up the road and through the square, the estate agent chatting to the vendors. We were ushered into a large office and introduced to the notaire. Marie-Claire positioned herself between Ray and myself and proceeded to translate at each stage of the proceedings. Various documents were exchanged between us all for signature, including the official statement that the property had been examined for termites and found to be free.

"Does this mean there is no woodworm?" I said to Marie-Claire

"Oh no, indeed no, there will be woodworm in your house most definitely, the whole of France is covered with woodworm, this only means no termites. It is a requirement on the sale of any property to have this certificate."

I wondered at this point how many woodworm we did indeed have, but it was quickly dismissed as we duly made our signatures and handed over the signed cheque for the remaining amount of French money to make the property ours. It was quite an informal affair; the vendors seemed pleased with the sale.

As we departed from the office they suggested we all sit in the square and participate in a celebratory drink. So there we were, sitting in the lovely square with sunlight beaming through the shady trees, trying to converse in French. Madame Vallade did try to help out a little with the odd English word here and there. Her son was actually working in England as a French teacher. I am sure she had quite a good understanding of English. Marie-Claire then said "au revoir" to all of us, returning to her office across the square.

We were then invited to the Vallades' house, which was in the same village, for refreshments before our taxi arrived. Monsieur Vallade explained that he had put in a planning application to extend the property. Knowing we had plans to enlarge it ourselves, Ray tried to convey that we would be keen to see the drawings.

Their house was reached by climbing up steep steps via a narrow pedestrian passageway. It had a charming wooden balcony which overlooked the whole town and the surrounding countryside. It was lovely sitting out on the shady balcony catching the breeze and sipping a cool drink. We were shown some very basic sketches of a plan to turn the workshop round the back of the cottage into a utility room, but no plans for the loft area. We kept these rough hand-drawn sketches, but as there were no official documents we did not know how far they had got with the Mairie for planning permission.

They also told us to expect a good walnut harvest from the trees situated at the far edge of the boundary. The nuts are picked in late October. It was interesting to learn that they had inherited the property while living and working in the Landes area, which is south of Bordeaux. They had rented it to tenants for the last five years and on retiring, had intended to move back into the property, hence their plans for enlarging it. Then they had had the chance to acquire their present property, with exceptional views, in this very desirable village. We later found out that our cottage had been on the market for a couple of years. I think by this time they were relieved to be selling and not have the worry of it. This explained why it appeared to be so neglected.

The time slipped by quickly until we had to say our farewells and make our way back to the square. The taxi swept us off to the station; the train arrived to the minute and we soon alighted at Angoulême station.

That evening we walked up to the old quarter of the town, which was full of character and history. We wandered around the quaint streets and chose a restaurant to dine and toast our success in acquiring the property. Unfortunately we neither had time nor transport to visit the cottage. That would have to wait to the following week.

The following morning at 7.30 a sleek, shiny TGV train pulled into the station and we arrived at the airport outside Paris within 2½ hours, the train only making one stop, at Poitiers. We sat in our obligatory reserved seats and enjoyed the comfort and speed that French trains have to offer. We returned to Bristol by air and arrived home late afternoon.

Only one week to go and we would be back again, finding out what we had let ourselves in for.

The ferry for the two-week trip crossed from Portsmouth to the French port of St Malo. We planned to stop one night half way down at a bed and breakfast. I did the usual preparation for this, checking out *chambre d'hôte* addresses. These are equivalent to small bed-and-breakfast overnight stops in private homes and are advertised and rated according to the book printed by the French Tourist Board. I decided on an address just outside Niort; it appeared to have plenty of garden space for easy parking.

The new trailer was made ready and packed. Protected by blue plastic covers and well roped down, it looked quite bulky, with odd lumps bulging from under the cover. The new bath had been placed in the bottom of the trailer and filled up with pillows, bedding etc. All the essential tools were placed around it, along with buckets and cleaning materials. Wooden slats had been slotted to the sides of the trailer for supporting the next layer, which was a door with bevelled glass on the top half. A double bed followed, along with the flatpack furniture. From friends we had acquired two small wooden-framed cottage armchairs. They had firm removable cushions for seats and back-supports, which I recovered with upholstery material. We manoeuvred the chair frames onto the rear seats of the car, while the cushions had been packed inside the trailer. Then numerous items were squeezed in around the frames. Needless to say the boot of our Peugeot 406 saloon was crammed to the very limit.

A large square carpet rug, stored in our loft from ages past, was rolled and wrapped in plastic; this would add some comfort to one of the rooms. It was placed on top of the covered trailer and well secured to the ladder rack along with a very high wooden step ladder, originally made by my father. It was very strong and sturdy and would enable us to reach the three-metre high ceilings. Lastly a couple of brooms were tied on and the strange looking trailer was ready. It was stacked to the absolute maximum height allowed by the ferry company.

The route to the ferry terminal was roughly a two-hour journey. The only obstacle was the climb out of the low-lying city of Bath. The best route was the slow haul up Limpley Stoke hill on the A36, which was a lower gradient than other routes but still meant a long pull in low gear. I sat with fingers crossed as we ascended. It was a two-mile climb to reach flat ground and I heaved a sigh of relief when we started to level out. Ray took the climb extremely slowly, dropping well back from the traffic ahead. Fortunately we did not have to stop and give the car and trailer the test of re-starting on a 1:5 gradient.

Our next breath-holding exercise was at the ferry terminal when we were pulled over and questioned as to what was in the trailer. I did have a list of contents ready to offer the customs people as a last resort in case they said "unrope it". This would not have been an option if we had wanted to sail that night. It had taken hours to rope the trailer to make it safe for its two-day journey. Customs gave us the all clear on our verbal itinerary and we were on board at last.

Embarking the next morning to bright skies and high

hopes, we set off, maps at the ready. The journey at that time was not so straightforward as it is now. The motorway section ended at Niort and we had to negotiate the centre of this large town, following all the signs. We had already made several stops at larger DIY hyperstores during the day. Ray had wanted to make notes of prices and check out availability of items we might need in the future. This knowledge would have a bearing on whether we had to bring certain materials for the restoration or purchase them in France.

When we arrived at our chambre d'hôte at six in the evening, the hosts seemed bemused at our trailer. We uncoupled it using a jockey wheel, as we needed the car to drive off and find a restaurant. We explained the purpose of our journey and that the contents of the trailer were for work on our newly-acquired property down in the south west. They enthused about our project and asked us many questions in French, which we tried to answer but not very successfully. They made us welcome and next morning, after a super *petit déjeuner* of bread, croissants and home-made jams, we set off again in high spirits.

We expected to arrive at the house early afternoon, thus giving us time to unload the trailer and car and prepare our bed for the night. On all subsequent visits we have done the journey within the day, arriving at around 5 pm after leaving the ferryport at nine. The first visit was different, as we knew it would take a while to get sorted out for the first night's stay, hence our plan for an overnight stop to ensure arrival earlier on the first day.

From Niort we headed south on the motorway in the

direction of Bordeaux. The sun shone and we could sense the rising temperature outside the car. The scenery began to open out once we entered Vendée country. White fluffy clouds gave way to clear blue skies on the horizon. Unripe fields of wheat stretched on either side of us as we rolled along a newly-opened stretch of motorway. We commented on the lack of other vehicles as we journeyed on and on; how different to England.

Once we turned off the motorway the scenery changed again and we saw the neat tidy rows of vines as we entered Pineau country. We had left the vast expanse of cornfields in the Charente and we could now distinguish new green shoots on the vines. The sun, now extremely hot in the clear blue sky, beamed down across the landscape. It all began to take on a different look as the countryside developed a more rolling nature. The small villages we were passing through seemed very sleepy and their sandy-coloured stonework reflected the heat; shutters were pulled half closed against the sun.

At one point, along a very straight stretch of road, Ray pulled off onto a safe verge and we decided on a short break. A photograph was taken of us alongside the trailer with its funny bulky contents and silly grins on our faces as we anticipated the excitement of arriving within the hour at our own French cottage. We had already stopped earlier at an Intermarché and purchased bread, milk and provisions for our arrival.

At last we were nearing our final destination. We passed very close to the village we had visited last week to do the signing with the notaire, then through the small village where we had been taken to see the property, opposite the lovely old twelfth century church and past the small restaurant with customers sitting outside on the terrace. We crossed over the river Dronne on the narrow bridge, closer and closer, almost there now. As we drove slowly through the hamlet our cottage came into view.

What a shock!

The anticipation and excitement we had felt over the last few months suddenly evaporated with the sight before us. Surely this was not what we had bought; it looked so different from the way we remembered it. Everywhere around the cottage was completely overgrown, and the hedge along the boundary trailed into the ditch. Shrubs sprouted out from all around the property, mingled with thigh-high grass. On our last viewing in February everything had been bleak and bare, but now it was bursting with greenery from all angles. There were weeds three feet high, and enormous molehills showed through the thin layer of stones around the front of the property.

We pulled onto the uneven tracks. The front lawn was now so overgrown you could not tell where it met the tracks round the back. Shrubs were completely buried in briars, some in flower trying to fight their way to daylight. The warmth of the sun shone down on us as we turned the key to open the faded front door. Slowly we stepped across the threshold.

Inside was dark and cool. Opening the tall shutters, we flung wide the windows to let out the tired, musty smell. We walked through the rooms and surveyed our new purchase. Left of the front door was entry to the shower room with wash-basin and bidet. These two tiny rooms would be the main objective of our first visit as we would be making them into one small area with just enough room for the new bath, wash-basin and low level toilet. The dividing wall between these rooms would be demolished after repositioning the existing water heater, which at present was suspended on it. If this plan was successful we would at least achieve the creation of a proper bathroom. After a hard day's work it is important to relax weary muscles in a nice warm bath so you can start afresh the following day.

Leading from the kitchen was another room at the front of the property which we hoped to make into a temporary sitting room. The other doorway from the kitchen led into a rear room which was dark as the window was on the north side, obscured by all the trees and shrubbery along the side of the house. From this room was the other rear room with horrid pink flock wallpaper. We had previously decided this would be the best room to make into our bedroom, as the window was to the south of the house and overlooked the garden.

There was certainly plenty to do, but now was not the time to dwell on what was facing us. Don't even think 'what next', just make a brave start! Back to the car and unhitch the trailer; start by bringing in the essentials. The hot water cylinder in the toilet was switched on. I tried not to notice the awful smell which came from this area. The adjacent shower-room floor was covered in dead insects and I thought no, it could wait. I began unpacking the crockery crates in the hope of finding the kettle. Ray had begun unloading the trailer and putting the tools into his workshop. I had hot water within half an hour and proceeded to wash down the tops of the units. The cupboards were so awful I did not want to put anything in them until they had been scrubbed clean. Within an hour Ray had assembled the flatpack table and chairs and was bringing in the double bed. This was assembled in the far rear room.

When the box containing the kettle was unpacked we stopped for a cuppa. Sitting on the lightweight chairs surrounded by boxes, suitcases and crates, we surveyed the view from the tall kitchen window and the bright yellow flowers of the crop in the field opposite. Suddenly we felt very close to all that beautiful countryside just a few yards away.

Eventually the initial frantic cleaning and unpacking ceased and some order was appearing. The table was laid up and a bottle of wine opened. There was an unsecured metal hob balanced on the row of tired-looking kitchen units. It had three gas rings and one electric plate. It would have originally worked from a 'gaz' container, no longer present. To my surprise the hot plate worked and with the aid of this I cooked omelettes. These were enjoyed with the crusty bread and selection of cheeses we had purchased earlier.

We looked towards the west through the open window and watched the sun slowly sinking. Minds diverted from the tasks ahead, we were just very thankful that we had successfully arrived intact with the loaded trailer. Tomorrow would be a fresh start.

Meeting the neighbours

We woke early the next morning to complete silence. On opening the shutters we could see the sun rising and hear the distant sounds of the countryside. It was Saturday, and we had decided to visit the largest supermarket we knew to purchase a cooker and fridge-freezer, coupling the empty trailer to the car so we could return with the appliances. Chances were, in a large town the assistants might speak English. We headed north to the city of Angoulême, a journey of one hour.

Perched high on the hillside, set in an industrial estate, was a very large supermarket complex containing covered shops and restaurants. It was aptly named Le Géant, and as the name implied it was gigantic and full of choice. We found an assistant who spoke a little English (he was seconded to us from the hi-fi area) and he demonstrated the appliances we were interested in. I chose a small free-standing electric cooker with four hotplates, a basic oven and warming drawer, a roomy fridge with a large deep-freeze compartment and a microwave which was on special offer, white with a yellow trim. I had decided the kitchen would be yellow and this model appealed rather than the plain white. It would be another three years before the kitchen was finally finished!

The young assistant was very helpful and explained the cooker and fridge were not in stock but had to be delivered direct from a central warehouse to our address. Fortunately we had brought a detailed map to show our whereabouts; as we were sixty kilometres away it appeared we would incur a delivery charge. To overcome this he told us to "wait and see" and disappeared for ages. When he returned he indicated that he had managed to avoid the charge as we were having two large appliances (delivery charges can be quite expensive in France). He told us to ring next Monday at 2 pm and he would confirm the delivery day, which he thought would probably be Friday.

It was now noon, so we went into the large restaurant area. We were astonished by the vast choice of tempting foods laid out before us. There were salads, cold meats, fish dishes and assorted cheeses accompanied with various mayonnaise sauces. Another counter was full of the most wonderful desserts. Wine was on tap from three barrels - rouge, blanc and rosé. Main courses were being served to choice, at very realistic prices. We discovered later that although this supermarket is closed all day Sunday to shoppers, the restaurant is open and people will travel for miles just for lunch.

We purchased a small, robust vacuum cleaner and could not resist a bike for less than £50. Lastly a large plastic garden table and four chairs, a must for eating outside, and again for £30 this was a bargain. Certainly it had paid us to go to a big store; the prices seemed low compared to England. We finished off by visiting the large food hall and buying all the provisions needed for the next week. The choice was immense, far superior to England.

Our Géant was on a large industrial estate with other large units. There were shops for wallpaper and paint, clothing, retailers for televisions and electrical goods and motor areas for tyres and car accessories. The only other shop we required that day was a *bricolage* (DIY store), and we found one on the estate called 'Mr Bricolage'. Where these differ from the ordinary bricolage is that they are hyperstores. We wanted to see what the cost of a new toilet and wash-basin would be and check out all the plumbing items. They had a toilet and cistern on special offer and we made notes of prices on various plumbing items.

One thing was becoming evident - purchasing a bath in England had not been a good idea. The taps for French baths are fixed to the wall and their baths have no holes for taps. After pondering and searching for ages we did find a set of taps that could be converted to suit our new bath. We purchased these along with some initial fittings to make a start the following week. Our time was now beginning to run out, and we had to be returning with our trailer full of purchases.

Sunday dawned, the day planned for the start. Ray was searching for the main feed into the bathroom area. The stop tap was just outside the front door and then it disappeared under concrete; although several pipes reappeared inside the bathroom and in the kitchen area, the main feed did not seem obvious. I decided to wash down the walls and paintwork of the room we were sleeping in. I made good progress perched on the tall wooden steps and had finished by lunchtime.

Ray was not doing so well, as he was still trying to locate the main water feed. On checking out the electrics he had found it was a complete mix up and various connections were very dodgy. I was instructed to be very careful about what I plugged in and where. Ray then gave up on finding the water feed, and said he would try to clear an area in the garden where we could put the new outside dining furniture. In the distance I heard the hum of the electric hover mower we had brought with us in the trailer.

Then a knock sounded at the open front door and the previous owner, Monsieur Vallade, appeared. I invited him in amidst the boxes and cleaning operations. He explained that he had found some extra keys to the property and had brought them over. Ray managed to find out from him where the main water feed was. This was some progress. We tried to explain to him our future plans regarding the layout of the rooms and alterations for the small bathroom area. I don't think he understood us. He wished us well and we bid "au revoir".

Deciding this would be a chance to stop and have some lunch, I prepared a quick snack. Ray had assembled the garden table and chairs in a cleared area of about four square metres just outside the bedroom window. "You did not clear very much" I said.

"We have a big problem, the grass has been left to get too long" he said. "I've just been speaking to Monsieur Vallade. He said we are going to need a much bigger mower. Then he wished me good luck!"

M Vallade was right. We were definitely going to need a lot of *bonne chance*. Apparently the mower had seized up because of the length of the grass; it was just too much for such a flimsy hover.

We sat in the sunshine and enjoyed the chance to have a break. The food was appetizing and the wine was going down a treat. We surveyed the scene from the garden area. The fallen apple tree was still evident alongside the tracks by the entrance. Near the far boundary, what had been the front lawn was a large laurel shrub growing into a row of other shrubs fifteen feet high, completely woven together with briars. We noticed from among the tall grass another fallen tree much larger than the apple tree, probably an oak. At this point, we could never imagine that this fallen tree would ever be removed. The whole garden looked so wild with nature taking over that it was not worth worrying about. We decided lunchtime was up and we returned inside.

I proceeded to wash down the room we were to use for a temporary sitting area. During the afternoon there came another knock and to our surprise Brian and Judy appeared. They were staying in their cottage just outside Ribérac and had remembered the date when we said we were coming to France. Because we had no phone connected they had decided to have a ride out and find us. Knowing the name of the hamlet and that we were the last house, they had found us without too much trouble. We were surprised, but so pleased to see them.

Entering the cottage, they observed the situation and the surroundings and were obviously very taken aback, realising we really had taken on a complete one hundred percent do-it-yourself project.

I made drinks while Ray proceeded to show them around. They were staying in their French home for a couple of weeks and gave us instructions to find them at their cottage. We agreed to visit Wednesday afternoon and stay for a barbecue.

Brian wanted to know just how we were going to set about improving the property and how long it would take before completion. We explained we were not putting any time limits on our expectations; after all it was a project for our retirement. Our son would be arriving the following Saturday for our last week's stay to assist with installing the new bathroom. Hopefully before his arrival we would have located the water feed and moved the water heater. We also told Brian that before our return we intended to clean down all the internal walls and paintwork, emulsion the ceiling of what would be our temporary lounge, fix up curtaining where necessary and commission the new bathroom area. That would probably be about the total sum of work we could realistically hope to cover in a fortnight. They wished us good luck and left us to continue with our cleaning efforts.

"We look forward to seeing you next week" said Brian. "We'll put a marker outside the front so you can find us."

On the Monday Ray located the main water feed and was

able to start. He took out the existing sink and replumbed it in the corner of the kitchen; luckily he was able to use existing pipes. This meant we would have washing facilities until the new installations in the bathroom area were completed. The old shower tray and bidet were pulled out.

Tuesday morning was spent trying to work out how to get the water-heater off the wall that was going to be demolished. Ray drained the system down and slowly we lowered it onto the heavy wooden steps. Eventually it was down, weighing an absolute ton and sitting in the middle of the kitchen floor. Exhausted, we retreated outside into the fresh air and decided to clear out the area we call the 'cycle shed' which had been described as a *remise* (shed) on details of the property. It was a solid stone lean-to adjoining the back of the house. It was two buildings really, divided by an internal wall. The larger area had been empty and Ray had unloaded all our materials and his tools into this space; it would now become his 'workshop'. The other was a darker area, which after our eyes became adjusted to the dark was seen to contain many unwanted items.

We decided to clear this valuable space and clean it up so that the garden tables and chairs and newly-acquired bicycle could be stored there, hence our nickname for it. Our plan also included rigging up a temporary light and site a temporary portable loo for use after the removal of the existing ancient and smelly toilet.

On Wednesday morning the plan for hauling the water heater two and half metres up the wall was put into action. The heater had been released from the previous position by roping and lowering it over copper pipes running around the ceiling of this area. We hoped that by the same method we could raise and fix it on the opposite wall. This did not work, and the piping gave way. Next plan was to gradually lift the heater step by step up the very sturdy wooden ladder we had brought with us. Once it was on the top step Ray would to lift it into place. Slowly we inched it up the ladder. (Had we known the excess weight was due to old limescale which had collected inside the heater, we would have emptied it.)

Finally, balanced on the very top of the ladder, Ray had to lift it a further half a metre to bolt it to the wall. I still don't know to this day how he found the strength to lift that heater and position the bolts single-handed. There was not enough room in the confined space for me to help with lifting. Ray was exhausted from struggling; the heater had to be secured on the wall by four 10 cm bolts.

Ray does not swear. Probably a working lifetime spent in customers' homes gave him strict control on his patience and verbal expressions. I am the one to say the occasional expletive. But I could sense the frustration growing. Eventually the bolts were fixed and tightened up.

I remarked "I don't know how you did that".

His reply, which contained much built-in anger at the situation, boiled down to the fact that if he had given up on this first major obstacle, then we might as well go home now and forget trying to do any more work. Putting it politely, I think he said, "We will have far more difficult problems than this to overcome if we are going to get this cottage sorted."

I was so relieved that the heater had finally been

reconnected on the wall. The task had seemed impossible without extra assistance, but we did it and it was the first of many impossible situations we had to overcome.

I think it had dawned on Ray just how arduous and onerous our project was going to be. Although he enjoyed practical individual projects, this was on a different scale. It was an enormous undertaking, which could only be tackled if it was planned and worked though at each stage.

I had envisaged Ray would be undertaking the project by himself, working in his own space and time. It was then that I knew I would have to be the 'mate' or 'gofer'; the cottage would be a lengthy project before it was completed. In order to speed things up he was going to need help, and I was the only help available.

Obviously I knew I would be working hard on the holiday visits to get the accommodation habitable, but only then came the full realisation that I would be spending the first five years of my retirement completely immersed in restoration work. We were definitely going to have to lighten up and laugh at situations that were going to arise all too often, as the future was going to involve us working very close together indeed.

Just as well we were going out for the afternoon. A breath of fresh air would do us good.

Taking the route recommended by Brian, we found ourselves in winding lanes threading through open countryside. Various individual properties were scattered amid the leafy scenery each with its own characteristic style of the region. Suddenly round a bend, in full view of the road, a mini château appeared, its four corners boasting pointed towers with an expanse of grey shuttered windows against the pale white stonework. Spacious gardens were beautifully tended with weed-free short grass and different varieties of straight tall ageless trees; what story was behind the origins of that house? Why was such a beautiful building in that spot? History would probably reveal it had been built for a bourgeois (middle class) family and then inherited by members of the same family over different generations. Now, to keep such a large home in pristine condition, it would be owned by a rich French businessman working in Paris or Bordeaux and using it as a weekend retreat.

As we drew near to our destination the countryside slowly changed from open rolling farm fields to clusters of small woods, interspersed with sunlit clearings.

We spotted Brian and Judy's tea towel signal swaying in the breeze over the narrow approach road. Their cottage was elevated and fronted the road. We turned into the driveway leading round to the rear. The noise of sawing was evident and an elderly man was operating a mini JCB. Two men were busy tidying an area which had become victim to the December tempest and we were introduced to the two workers, Denny, the older man, and Danny, his son.

At the rear of Brian's cottage, entry was through the kitchen leading to a hallway where the new oak staircase was being varnished by Judy.

"Hi there" she greeted us. "You found us OK? We are very tucked away amid forests and narrow lanes. Welcome to our haven or heaven, or should I say home of never ending jobs." She put down her paintbrush and laughed at Brian, who had been clearing his loft area and was covered in dust, fluff and cobwebs.

"Let me get you a glass of wine, we can go outside after you've seen around the place" she said. Turning left we entered an enormous lounge area. The height was easily seven metres to roof level; the undersides of the tiles showed between the rafters. A magnificent beam cut from a whole oak tree was suspended across the entire width of the room just above head height. The loft area over the hall and downstairs bedrooms was visible from the lounge, with protective wooden slats along the side of the gallery. Brian explained that the staircase had been recently installed by a local French carpenter. Previously the only access to the exposed open area had been via a ladder.

I observed Ray looking at the beam across the lounge and the natural stone wall behind the large white fireplace; bags of character boasting exposed beams and stone walls. I could sense his admiration of the traditional French-style room. Our cottage could never match that ambience. Even after the massive amount of work that was going to be involved with our retirement project, our property was never going to resemble the quaintness and agelessness that room had to offer. A sudden feeling of regret flooded over me. What if I had made the wrong decision in persuading him to buy our cottage? Perhaps I had been wrong, and we should have waited to find another property.

Then I remembered that our house was much smaller. Brian's had three downstairs bedrooms as well as all the space in the large gallery area; he had required a large property to accommodate his family and friends during the summer months. We did not need a spacious property and it had been hard enough to find our little house. Indeed we had turned down some very choice properties on account of their size. No, think positive, remember all the sensible reasons we had decided to choose our small house.

We passed a relaxing afternoon in their company. True to their promise made on the ferry last February, they took us on a short car journey to the déchetterie and the local bricolage in Ribérac, where we would shop in the future for many of our DIY products.

Denny and Danny were leaving when we returned from our trip. We told them of our grass problems and they promised to pay us a visit to help clear the garden before we left.

We sat drinking wine in the garden enjoying the barbecue. It was good to chat with them about their plans; a new roof next year, and if funds would allow, a swimming pool, mainly for the enjoyment of their sons and daughters, who would stay in their cottage in the summer months along with the grandchildren.

Judy and Brian still had plenty of jobs to do to realise their dream cottage. Originally it had been a farmhouse with a large barn which still contained the old wooden stable partitions for the animals; the house was around 150 years old. The logs from the fallen trees would be stored in the barn for burning on their log-burning stove. Brian was planning to install radiators so he could heat the cottage to spend time there in the winter months. Soon it was time to say our au revoirs. They would be returning to England the following week.

On our return, our cottage felt a little chilly in the early May evening. I surveyed the small room which we had made into a temporary sitting room. The rug covered the dirty floorboards and cheered it up. I sat in the cottage chair by the window facing west and surveyed the deepening red sky, a sign of a fine day tomorrow. Our plans for the next day involved Ray doing further checks on the electrics.

Although we were up very early, the next day passed quickly. Ray wired in a new cooker cable from the meter box, this being positioned on the wall next to where the cooker would sit. Luckily the meter box was in the kitchen. On testing out the electrics, some proved to be lethal. The fat original old-fashioned plugs were OK, but the extra sockets and lighting recently added in the small bathroom area were not compliant with regulations. A rewire was essential, but we had not anticipated the urgency.

I finished removing the paper in the rear north room; it was too early to know exactly what this room would be used for. I discovered what looked like a damp patch under the window which later only proved to be algae from old wallpaper and was easily washed off. I then began cleaning in the kitchen area in preparation for the delivery of the cooker the following day.

The afternoon sunshine beckoned, and I found the spade we had brought among the basic garden tools and began to remove some of the molehills from the front gate. Noticing a heavy scent in the air, I realised it came from some beautiful deep red roses surrounding the wrought iron gate and frame. There was another climbing rose bush around the front door; masses of deep red scented roses were bursting out and clinging around the wall to the front of the house.

The privet hedge running alongside the boundary was massively overgrown, the weight pulling it downwards into the deep ditch. These soakaway ditches were to the front and side boundaries. It reminded me of the story of Sleeping Beauty; impenetrable hedges and briars to be fought off before entry, years of neglect having created a wilderness. It would need more than a prince with a magic sword to cut through our jungle. It would take an electric hedge cutter, loppers and a large pair of secateurs. Our newly-cut small square patch round the back where we put the new garden table and chairs looked so silly, but it was a start.

On the Friday a delivery van arrived at the scheduled time; the driver performed the preliminary handshake which is customary in France. He inspected the area where we indicated the appliances should stand; he seemed in agreement and proceeded. The paperwork was confirmed and the cooker was positioned, along with the fridge freezer. We all shook hands again and he departed. We could now turn off our portable car cooler box, which had been working flat out since our arrival to keep abreast of the hot weather preserving milk, butter, cheese and meat. Before leaving home Ray had made a purpose-built box to house a small transformer, enabling the cooler box to run from mains electricity.

One full week had past and we had only accomplished

what seemed a very minor amount of change. We had moved the water heater from the wall soon to be demolished. Two rooms had been washed down from ceiling to floor and wallpaper had been removed from the rear north room. The kitchen was being scrubbed in stages. We had placed the small round table and chairs in one corner; the original sink from the small bathroom had been replumbed in the other corner behind a temporary screen. At least we could wash ourselves until the new one was installed. A temporary portable loo had been placed in the 'cycle shed' ready for when the old toilet and cistern was removed.

Success with the new cooker and at last, after managing with one small hot plate, I could now produce the usual 'cordon bleu' meals we were used to! Anyway the chops and two veg went down well after last week's succession of various omelettes accompanied with bread and wine.

We set off early to Angoulême. The previous Saturday we had seen a special offer on bathroom equipment so with a long list of plumbing fittings, including the required lengths of copper piping, we headed back to Mr Bricolage. The bathroom offer was not available and had been replaced by another special. We have long since learnt in France that if you see anything on promotion, buy it. Do not wait and expect to purchase it another day. The new special was a white sink with pedestal, toilet, lid and cistern inclusive of taps all for a bargain price.

By now it was midday and the shop was closing for two hours until two o'clock. We still had the long list of fittings to purchase, so we went back to the mall to have lunch with the other French customers who were stopping for their obligatory two-hour lunch. A choice of three restaurants and they were filling up quickly. After our meal we still had to wait until the DIY store reopened, so we stocked up with a week's provisions in the large grocery store which, luckily, did not close for the two hours.

Our son Paul was due in at Angoulême station on the TGV at 14.45, having taken only 2½ hours from Paris airport. At 15.00 I managed to contact him by mobile to say we were still in the process of fixing a newly-acquired double ladder to the roof rack. The list of fittings had proved a nightmare. Being in metric they did not compare to English sizes. All the packets were written in French, which made looking for all the individual pieces so frustrating. Paul's train had arrived on time - French trains are never late - and he was waiting at the station. Not to worry, he was having a beer in the station restaurant. His only complaint was the heat.

Fully loaded with a new ladder and copper pipe on the roof rack and boxes full of sanitary equipment along with a week's groceries in the car boot, we collected Paul from the station. We sped along back to our cottage with the car's air conditioning working well. Paul admired the countryside with its rolling fields of bright yellow rape seed (*colza*) alongside fields of green corn; he commented on the tightly-closed shutters against the heat of the afternoon sun. Passing through small villages we came closer to home. Entering our hamlet we reached the last small house on the left, and he immediately expressed amazement at the state of the property. We had told him many times it was a long-term retirement project, but I don't think he expected it to be so bad. After his initial shock he happily accepted the makeshift blow up mattress in the temporary sitting room, his bed for the week. He had travelled light with only old spare clothes for the dirty, messy work ahead of him.

We all freshened up before setting off to a local restaurant, where it was easy to unwind sampling the local cuisine and a bottle of *vin de pays*. Soon we were relaxing after such a frantic day. Paul was enthusing with us about the plans for the small cottage. By now he too was visualising the finished project and obviously the prospect of bringing friends with him to enjoy holidaying in France.

Sunday was demolition day. By 10 am the partition wall was a pile of rubbish being energetically shovelled out in rubble bags. The toilet and cistern had been trashed, along with the awful smell.

Sitting in the garden, we enjoyed a coffee break at the new table. A discussion on the loft area prompted us to take some time out to explore entry to the grenier. The new ladder was split into two sections, one part leaning up over the cycle shed and the other half over the sloping roof. We looped it over a hook set in the tiles under a small doorway to the loft and I followed the men up the ladder. Ray pushed the bolt away opening the hatch door. I volunteered to go in first, being the smallest.

Sunlight streamed into the open doorway to reveal a scene which was not at all what I had been expecting. A very thick central beam supported the roof running from the front of the cottage to the back. Two more beams ran either side of the central one, but at a lower level. Across the house from one side to the other were two rows of iron bars at knee height which connected into strong-looking side beams. The floor was covered in thick glass fibre. I pulled back the edge of this covering to reveal floorboards which looked fairly safe to walk on, so I climbed over the hatch ledge and stood inside the loft. It was relatively free of the cobwebs which I had imagined would be everywhere. There was no felting under the tiles. The only evidence of wildlife was wasps' nests on the underside of the tiling. These nests were round, flat and small, the largest approximately six inches wide, with many wasps tending young inside them. Once the opening had exposed daylight, the wasps began flying in and out. They did not seem to worry about us. Ray and Paul ventured over to the far side, climbing over the knee-high iron bars, and began to take measurements.

The area was split into three sections by the two iron rods at three-metre intervals. We measured how much head height we had before the roof sloped away to the sides. The right-hand side the roof, which covered the downstairs bathroom, protruded with a separate tiled area. In this space was a large concrete tank which we presumed had once contained water. Originally, when the cottage was built, this would have been the only source of water, pumped up from the well at the side of the house.

Our hopes of future expansion into this loft area seemed promising. There was head height in the centre; the depth of space would provide enough space for an extra bedroom and a more spacious bathroom. The only problem we could see were the iron bars, at knee height, which would have to be removed.

We returned to remove the last of the rubble from the bathroom area and at lunchtime we returned to relax in the garden. Discussions continued on how to best use the loft space and who to consult about the removal of the iron rods. At present these stopped anyone walking across the area and split the loft into three sections. The roof was ten metres from front to back and eight metres in width; a lot of area would be lost at the sides due to the slope of the roof. Plenty to think about, but the discovery of an existing solid wood floor over the whole area was a great bonus.

Obviously a staircase was required from one of the downstairs rooms to gain entry. Siting this would be an important decision. Now was not the time; the installation of the new bathroom was the priority.

The bathroom had pretty patterned Italian tiles half way up the wall and around the shower area. We decided to carefully remove the ones from the shower area so as to reuse them around the new wash-basin. This was managed successfully and I was given the job of removing the old grouting. Using our Workmate to clamp the tiles I could then remove the old plaster with an electric grinding tool. Sparks flew everywhere, but after three hours of dusty work I had cleaned up thirty tiles for reuse later that week.

The room was now completely empty. With the partition wall removed it left an L-shaped area. The bath was retrieved from the workshop and tried in the space. Just as the plan showed, it was a very tight fit, but there was just enough room to squeeze past at the side. The sink would fit in alongside the bath under the small window and the toilet would be positioned using the same sewerage exit. The plumbing could now commence in the morning. We had done well that Sunday.

First thing Monday, Paul decided he would cycle the three kilometres on the newly-purchased cycle to the small town of Saint Aulaye. He intended to get fresh croissants and bread for breakfast. While I waited outside for him to return I wandered a little way up the white lane. I turned and the early rays of sunlight from behind me shone onto the house opposite. It had bright red shutters and the garden was full of roses. Roses were all around the house as well; climbers in beautiful colours fastened to straining wires enhancing the steps leading up to the doorway. We knew the owner was Madame Moyrand from conversations with our sellers.

Realising she was in her garden, walking up and down the rows of vegetables to the side of the property, I thought it timely to introduce myself. Trying to remember my lessons in French conversation from night school, I made my best efforts. Although she spoke only in French, I managed to gather some of the information she was imparting. It appeared there was another English couple who owned a cottage in our hamlet. They had asked her to explain that they wanted us to visit when we arrived; she believed they were in residence.

She spoke in precise, slow French and when I looked at her blankly she would helpfully try to tell me in another way. Her full name was Marie-Odette Moyrand and she had two daughters, one living in the last (and oldest) house in the village. She worked at the University of Bordeaux and often travelled to England, where she lectured at the University of the West of England in Bristol - what a coincidence. Her other daughter worked in Belgium and only visited occasionally but we would meet her in September. I said I would speak to her again before we left at the end of the week.

Meanwhile Paul had arrived home and with Ray had started breakfast, tucking into the croissants.

"Where have you been? You're missing this super French food. We've left you a croissant" Ray said. I told them I had held a conversation with the neighbour who lived opposite and what she had said about our English neighbours.

"I don't think we'll have time to do that" he said. "We are really pushed to finish the bathroom." Even so I was determined that I would make the visit, even if I had to go alone.

Work progressed up to midday, when Ray realised extra plumbing fittings were required in another metric size. Paul and I went off to the bricolage at Ribérac to search for them. When we arrived it was still lunchtime and of course the shop was shut until two. We had a drink in a local café and waited. Eventually we purchased what we could; still some parts short, we returned home by half past three. Deciding to try the bricolage at Chalais, the next closest town to us, we found the parts there, but by the time we returned it was too late to fit them.

So the week progressed and by Thursday it was all coming together. The bath, sink and toilet were all in position and Paul offered to emulsion the ceilings. This proved fruitless, because the French paint he was using was rubbish. The consistency was so weak that it failed to cover the old foam ceiling tiles. Abandoning this, he went outside to hack away at some of the shrubbery in the garden. We decided we would have to bring over our own paint for all the future work in the cottage.

On Friday the two men we had met at Brian's cottage arrived. As promised they had come to see if they could help with getting the grass to ordinary cutting level. Danny (the son) commenced strimming and continued for three hours. He was covered in thick overalls because of the possibility of stones springing back from the heavy strimmer. He was also wearing wellington boots in case of snakes in the long grass. He was sweating in the heat as it was very hot again; he was grateful to stop to cool off and continued after a salad lunch and cold drinks.

It took six hours of continuous strimming to clear the area. By then it looked very different - you could actually see the start of the driveway, the fallen apple tree and some of the shrubs. We discussed the possibility of keeping the grass cut and they agreed to keep it under control on a maintenance contract. They would remove the fallen apple tree and the other large tree that was lying in our acre. We were very grateful to them, as no way did we have the tools to tackle that job; we felt relieved to think that the grass would be kept cut until we returned in September.

That evening we moved the garden table to a cleared area and sitting amid the long grass strewn around us we enjoyed our meal in the warmth of the evening sunshine. We had one more day left, which would be spent getting everything packed up. The trailer would return to England containing all the tools Ray had brought to carry out the jobs. Obviously it would be a lot lighter on the return journey, but we had purchased a few boxes of French wine at the Géant the previous weekend to take back. We decided that the two original doors from the bathroom could be worked on at leisure in England. These solid wood doors would be taken back to their natural state and stained; eventually the spare one could be used in the loft area to one of the new rooms, thus keeping the original doors in the cottage where possible.

Most of Saturday was occupied with tidying and sorting; again it was a hot day and by the afternoon it was twenty-seven degrees in the shade. We had arranged to have a meal that evening at a restaurant we had come across on the journey back from Judy and Brian's. It was on a quiet country road and was a converted barn with a chambre d'hôte alongside. We had reserved a table for three for eight that evening. I had done most of my packing by 4 pm, so I decided that before dinner I would seize the chance of visiting the people at the end of the village.

Their pale blue shutters were open and a car was parked outside, so I knew there was a good chance they were home. There was no visible front door, only a side gate with a large bell. I pulled the chain and it clanged. I could hear voices coming from the garden behind the doorway and shortly it was opened by a slim, active-looking gentleman with a warm smile. I guessed he was in his late sixties or early seventies.

"I've come from the house at the end of the village," I

said. "We're returning tomorrow but I felt I must come and introduce myself before we go."

"Yes of course, I'm pleased you have" he said. "I'm Terry. Come in meet my wife Ingrid."

He indicated seats and a table in the centre of a walled garden. It was like stepping into a perfect English country garden with closely-mown, weed-free grass with stone edged borders and central flower beds. Roses were climbing over empty low-roofed barn buildings, forming a boundary on one side; around the area were many flowering shrubs. A profusion of colour was everywhere and there was the calming sound of running water in a small water fountain nearby. I could see that behind the shelter of the wall, the garden went on forever with many tall trees and intricate little paths.

"Please join us for a drink in the garden" said Terry. "We hoped you might have time to visit. We knew your cottage had been sold at long last. Afraid it needs a lot doing though. What are your plans? "

I was introduced to Ingrid and her friend Olivia. I joined them and a pot of tea was produced, along with home-made jam and a slab of Madeira cake. I learned that they were staying in France until early July. They lived in a small village in the Yorkshire Dales and would be returning to France in September, when they made me promise to come back to see them again with Ray. I said I would look forward to a proper tour of their garden on my next visit. We chatted for about an hour and I said I must get back to do more packing ready for our long journey back to the ferryport on Sunday.

I was so pleased I had managed to meet them. They were a lovely couple and made me feel so welcome, and they had wanted to hear about our plans to refurbish the cottage. They knew our house well; it had been inhabited by a Polish couple who had lived there for many years. Eight years previous Terry and Ingrid had purchased a surplus of wood-burning logs before the couple returned to Poland to live out their days in their native country. The property had been rented to them from our vendors; then after a succession of tenants it was sold to us. Ingrid and Terry were well aware of the condition and all the work that was needed to make it habitable. They wished me good luck and conveyed their wishes to Ray, who they looked forward to meeting in September.

I viewed our cottage walking back through the village. It looked no different from the way it had on our arrival, except for the grass lying around everywhere exposing more tangled shrubs. Perhaps there were a few less weeds and molehills amongst the front stones.

Inside however there had been definite progress, and tonight I was going to have a bath in the new bathroom. I surveyed the new bath and wash-basin with sparkling chrome taps and the newly-positioned splash back tiles with a new mirror and shelf. In the far corner was the 'no smelling' brand new low-level suite. The original water heater was now repositioned up above.

The walls were still in a rough state and would have to be papered and emulsioned on our next visit. The existing pretty wall tiles were now clean. We had thrown out the worn existing floor covering, exposing a concrete floor. We would cover this with new floor tiles on our next visit. What more could have been achieved in two weeks? The kitchen area was clean and the old worktops had been scrubbed down several times. The original temporary wash-basin had now been removed from the corner and the area tidied up. Flowers from the garden were on the table. It was beginning to feel like our cottage.

On my return from Ingrid and Terry I had seen Madame Moyrand out in her garden again. She called out and beckoned me into the very large barn building at the side of her house. It was massive and contained an assortment of gardening implements. She was trying to tell me to put down *souris poudre* (mice powder) and she gave me some packets. Although I could only get the gist of what she was saying it seemed important to leave these packets around the house.

We set off to the restaurant. Entry was into a large open area with stone walls and a balcony around the top of a staircase; it was full of atmosphere with widely-spaced tables. Our host, the wife of the chef, indicated we could choose where we wished to sit. Enjoying a fixed-price menu of five courses we ordered a bottle of Bordeaux wine to accompany the meal. We toasted ourselves on a successful two weeks and all we had achieved. Totally relaxed for the rest of the evening, we digested all the delicious French cuisine.

Our return was through dark country lanes back to the cottage. It was pitch black, but as we alighted from the car the sky was brilliantly lit with stars. I had never seen so many. The more you gazed, the more you saw; there seemed to be millions. Paul started calling out the famous ones. "That's the Plough over there and that's the Seven Sisters" he said. It was awesome, but it would be only the first of many starry nights we would experience, living deep in the countryside where no town lights mar the night sky.

Spiders, staircases and secrets

The summer months passed so slowly, and the wait for our return to the cottage seemed endless. The list of items to purchase was undertaken at once. Numerous items were stored in the spare bedroom for packing in the trailer on the September visit. The list was gradually shortening, but then other items were added, as more ideas emerged for future visits.

Ray sketched out the loft, showing the iron rods that blocked a free walkway across the area. We intended to have a larger bathroom (complete with an independent shower) which would give us room to move around freely. Although extremely pleased with our efforts to date on improving the existing bathroom, we visualized more floor area where you did not knock your backside against the wall when you bent over to wash your hair. A bedroom was outlined on the plan at the opposite end to the bathroom. The space in the middle would be a bonus; a walk-in-wardrobe or just an open-plan area.

The two doors we had brought back from the bathroom area were stripped back to the original wood and then taken to a local firm for an acid dip to remove final traces of paint; after staining and varnishing they were ready to return. Many diagrams were drawn with a view to positioning a staircase that would eventually lead to the loft area. Contact was kept with the men who had promised to keep the garden under control. Although we were both in full-time work, any spare time was generally absorbed by discussion on the cottage, with a constant flow of new ideas. With so much restoration and only a visit twice a year, it was important we had a plan for each occasion.

The trailer was finally loaded, though several attempts were made before all the items fitted. If we thought our first trip had a full load, it was nothing compared to this effort. It was securely covered against the elements with plastic covers and strong roping binding it up like a ball of wool. As usual Ray's tools had filled the bottom of the trailer. Wooden slats were placed on the top edge to form a base for the returning doors; this formed a nice large area to stack lots of other items up the height limit. There was one single solid wooden wardrobe (filled with extra bedding) and a very large solid wood bureau.

The dozen long planks of wood for skirting, along with ten three-metre lengths of picture rail, were tightly wrapped in separate plastic covers and placed on top of the wrapped trailer. These two large, heavy bundles of wood were tied to the ladder rack along with three apple trees. After the wood and the trees had been added we had exceeded the 1.83 metres permitted height for the ferry and we were just above the measuring line allowed at the ferry terminal. Eyebrows were raised and shoulders shrugged, but, very thankfully, we were allowed through the barrier.

The heavily-filled trailer attached to the towbar was a constant concern when we faced a steep incline. We took the same route as our May trip, driving out of Bath up the Limpley Stoke valley. Slowly we crawled up the hill with fingers crossed, achieving a good run at the 1:5 gradient. For the two-mile stretch Ray controlled the gears so that we kept a nice constant speed. The slow climb safely behind us, the only other driving problem would be the ramp at the ferry and the Nantes Bridge.

Everything went well the next day; the night ferry crossing had been calm and the French roads were traffic free. The Nantes Bridge loomed before us high in the sky. Thanks to clever design by the French it allowed a good run before a slow climb. It was situated on the periphery road around Nantes and once over the summit we turned off to join the motorway which headed south to Bordeaux.

We arrived around 5 pm, and as on our first visit our arrival gave us a shock. Everything looked so different from the way it had when we had left back in the spring. The grass was burned brown through being scorched by the summer sunshine, though it was nothing like as long as on the first visit. The men had obviously been cutting it. As promised, they had removed the fallen apple tree and stacked the logs in a tidy pile in the barn. The huge pampas grass shrub had been removed, which opened up the area. A very large tree which had fallen in the previous December tempest was still lying between the high dried-out shrubs, from which protruded very thick and healthy briars.

The surrounding crops which we had left in May were now replaced by maize at eye level. This all added up to a complete change of scenery, making everything look different.

We entered the cottage. There were dead insects everywhere and dust spiders high on the ceiling, but no evidence of dead mice. The powders had all been eaten but they must have returned outside to die. We opened up all the windows after throwing back the shutters. Fresh air and evening sunlight flooded in and we set to work washing down the tops and sweeping out all the dead flies and wasps.

After a couple of hours the fridge was up and running with the groceries unloaded. The bed had been made and our suitcases brought in and unpacked. We showered in the new bathroom. After unhitching the trailer, the tail end of the car came up at least twenty centimetres.

Off to the café on the corner, where the whole square was alive with people sitting at the tables under the trees, which were lit up with small lights interspersed in the branches ready for dusk. It was marvellous to relax and unwind after the tensions of the journey.

We enjoyed the warm summer breeze and drank our wine, closely guarding the bread basket in case it was whisked away before we had finished the delicious French bread. It was so great to be back again, even with all the work we had planned to do on this second visit. It was such a pleasure to be in the area among all the people enjoying their evening. Obviously most of them were tourists, but we were the lucky ones as we could look forward to being able to stay longer than a fortnight's holiday. But that was a long way off. We returned to fall into bed and wondered what our first day at the cottage would bring.

It was Friday morning when we set off to the local market in Ribérac. At 8.30 it was already busy. A brightly-coloured stall was selling tablecloths depicting scenes of the area; geese, sunflowers, vines and grapes. Another displayed furniture and mattresses, while second-hand lawnmowers and garden spades were arranged on the corner of the square. Turning the corner, dresses, skirts and tops swayed in the breeze, along with a fitting room - the large white van behind the stall.

Leading into the very heart of the market we found masses of fresh produce displayed. There were wonderful fish counters with very fresh fish of various species displayed on beds of ice. They included large lobsters and crabs along with crevettes (very large pink prawns). The bags of snails (which were alive) did not appeal very much. Hurrying past that stall, we purchased two bottles of Pineau apéritif, one rouge the other blanc. It was produced at a vineyard only a few kilometres away from our village. Two punnets of strawberries were added to our basket before we headed to the market café for a croissant and coffee.

People had come from far and wide to visit the Friday morning market. There was such variety - shoes, hats, underwear, linen, bedding, pots and pans, knives and belts. Various sizes of framed prints showed local scenes for the tourists beside an uncovered area displaying all manner of hand-painted glazed pottery. We purchased a pitcher for wine and a matching fruit bowl. As we made our way through the now packed market we could hear the strains of French accordion music coming from a stall selling compact discs.

We reached our car and wove out of the area among the pedestrians who were still arriving. By midday all the stalls would be cleared away and the area hosed down; it would be as if no market had existed. No rubbish would be left, not one scrap. Everything would be taken away, along with the white vans, until next Friday when it would return and the whole process would be repeated.

By midday we too had left Ribérac, our shopping completed from the large supermarché, homeward bound with groceries for the coming week. We sat out in the garden enjoying our baguettes and pâtisseries. The sun shone and we felt happy, so happy, to be back again. In the afternoon we had to unpack the trailer, find homes for all the tools in the workshop and untie and stack bundles of wood.

Ray assembled the workbench he had inherited from my father and sited it in his workshop. It was very solid, having been hand-made by Dad many years ago. We had brought it over in the bottom of the trailer. Another item we had managed to squeeze on the trailer had been a lovely old wrought-iron wine rack. It had four shelves, each holding four bottles, and a small wooden top on which we placed the fruit bowl. It helped cheer the kitchen up, and was already holding a nice selection of local wine.

On Saturday afternoon we received visitors; Denny and Danny, the two men who had been maintaining the garden, turned up to see us. They wanted to know if we were pleased with the clearance and offered to inspect the loft and look at the situation regarding the iron rods and the beams. We arranged the ladders over the cycle shed roof so they could enter the loft space, leaving them to see what they made of the situation. After the inspection we sat under the shade of the cherry tree with iced drinks and discussed possibilities. They were familiar with the design of iron rods suspended between beams from Guernsey, where they had lived and worked before settling in France. They offered to make enquiries locally about installing dormer windows and get a price for building a bespoke staircase from a local carpenter. They then came inside the house and did measurements of the rooms, paying attention to the height of the ceilings. Ray offered the sketches he had made of various places to site the staircase.

During the first week a lot of time was spent working on the bathroom area. Plastic floor tiles were laid on the exposed concrete floor and the ceiling was given a coat of white emulsion. We decided that the plaster on the walls was in such a poor state it would need to be covered with blown vinyl paper. A top coat of paint was given to the small window before hanging the newly made curtains.

The next major job was to block off the empty space where one of the doorways had been removed. Originally there had been a doorway to each of the small rooms. On removal of the partition wall we now only needed one doorway to our bathroom. The idea was to permanently fix a half-bevelled glass door we had brought over from England on the first visit. Instead of making a proper window frame and building up a partition (which would be very time-consuming) this idea would suffice; also it would let light from the bathroom into the small hallway.

A third door we had taken back to England had been found abandoned in the cycle shed. On measuring it we found it should have been hung between the small lobby and the kitchen. At some point the tenants had removed it, but luckily they had not used it for firewood. The newly-treated door was returned to its original position. This was a great improvement and stopped the toilet door from being seen from the kitchen.

Still having a very temporary kitchen arrangement, I put only a few items into the old cupboards. Although we had not found any mice, I was not happy about using these cupboards. I scrubbed them out and lined them with brown paper, but I still fancied they smelt and preferred to keep items like fruit and vegetables in a new vegetable rack and the bread and cakes in my own tins on top of the work surface.

We received a visit from our neighbour opposite, bringing us *pommes de terre* from her garden and enormous, wonderful-tasting tomatoes. These had been grown outside in full sunshine; they were delicious, especially in salads. Her daughter, who accompanied her, was visiting from Brussels where she worked. She spoke fluent English (as well as several other languages) and had come over to help us all have a three-way conversation. Madame Moyrand explained that her brother Philip, who lived in Normandy, was married to an English lady called Sophie. They visit her twice a year in May and October, so in the spring, if we were at our cottage, we would be invited for apéritifs. Sophie would interpret our conversations.

Marie-Odette reminded us that our *noyers* (walnut trees) would soon be ready for harvesting. As we would have left before this date we invited her, along with the previous owners, to collect all the nuts they wanted. She said she would contact them.

On nights when we did not eat in the garden we sat in the kitchen at the small table with the windows wide open enjoying the sunset. As it was September it would begin to darken around nine (still later than England, due to being one hour forward). The problem we found with eating our meals in the garden area was that with only the one door to the property, everything had to be carried around to the back. Morning coffee and afternoon tea was OK, but the three-course meal evening meal meant a lot of transporting food and crockery.

After working hard during the day we would stop around six to shower, change and prepare the meal. We looked forward to unwinding in the evening with a really enjoyable meal. There was plenty of choice; tender cuts of meat and the duck breasts were so easily bought at local shops. After the main course we would have a selection of French cheeses, along with a baguette accompanied by the wine. We would try a different variety each week. We'd take a rest before dessert, then enjoy a delicious French pastry, individually chosen at the baker's that morning.

Following the evening meal, if we had not lingered too long, we would take a stroll. We had a good choice. The shortest amble would be turning left from the front gate up to the iron cross. It was approximately 500 metres to the cross. There was a slight incline on the journey and on turning to come back you faced the sunset and surveyed the open fields before you. Well back from the road were two dense copses either side. We had often caught glimpses of deer in these woods. Laid out before us, as we descended, was our small hamlet nestling in all this beautiful scenery with a backdrop of rolling hills in the direction of Chalais.

Our favourite stroll was through Haut Bois itself. Passing the neighbour on our side of the road we would encounter the barking of their small poodle; we calmed her down by stroking her through the wire fencing encasing the property. It was a two-storey house, probably built after ours with newly-replaced dark wooden shutters and a large workshop to the side.

One evening we had said our bonsoirs when we were called into an area on the opposite side of the road. It was an enclosed vegetable garden to the left, with to the right at least a dozen assorted breeds of chickens, plus four ducks, two geese and two peacocks. The lady introduced herself as Yvette and described it as her *ménagerie*. Opposite her house was another property looking very similar to ours, as it seemed very solidly built. It bore a number 74 in blue and white enamel, like the street numbers you see in Paris.

Next was a large single-storey house facing onto a large wide courtyard where tractors turned into barns through a rear entrance. This was the home of the beef farmer, Monsieur Sautet. He owned most of the *vaches* (cows) seen grazing in the surrounding fields.

At the far edge of the courtyard was the house of Monsieur Raynaud, the arable farmer who cut our meadow. It was very impressive, a two-storey house with a high sloping roof. Black wrought-iron railings enclosed a large front garden. Opposite the farmer's dwelling was another large, long and low dwelling belonging to the grandparents of the couple who lived in the small cottage after Yvette's house.

Finally on our side was the oldest house in the hamlet, which belonged to the daughter of our neighbour Marie-Odette. It was a lovely stone-built cottage full of character, with enormous barns to the rear. Opposite was Ingrid and Terry's cottage, which I had visited in the spring. This was the last of the individual properties scattered along the village.

The road continued on in the direction of Chalais, but just after leaving our small hamlet there was a very sharp turn to the left. Around the corner behind a tall wall was a beautiful old building like a mini château. The entrance between two stone pillars led into a courtyard out of sight behind a large barn with a newly-restored roof. Opposite was a beautiful thirty-metre wide lake with lily pads from which we could hear the croaking of frogs on warm evenings. After peering into the water watching large trout swimming, we would stroll round the pond and then sit on a bench admiring the view of the house. The closely-cut grass surrounding the house and pond added to the cultured look at the end of the village. Tall trees skirted the fields opposite and we would walk up the road to the end of the boundary of the manor house and sit on a stone seat, where we watched the sun setting over the surrounding countryside.

The third walk was a sharp turn right on leaving our front gate down the white lane. Our neighbour called this walk 'Le Grand Tour'. As yet we had not had the time to embark on this walk; the pleasure was still to come.

During the first week, while Ray was working on blocking off the old doorway entrance, I removed the wallpaper in the kitchen and washed down the walls. It certainly freshened up the area; the old blackened floorboards were scrubbed again, but they remained the same colour with years of ingrained dirt. I sanded down the bare wood on the window frames and gave them a coat of primer. The tall windows (made up of six separate panes in each frame) urgently needed the glass to be re-puttied to make them watertight. Recently, in a heavy storm, the shutters had been open and the rain had poured in through the gaps where putty was missing. The outside shutters on the front of the house were also in a bad way, devoid of paint and split in various places. It was a case of finding time to restore them.

We had brought three apple trees with us to plant; one was a Bramley cooking apple. In France you can buy only Granny Smith apples, which have some degree of sharpness for making traditional English apple pies, but they are nowhere near as good as Bramleys. One afternoon we tried to dig holes to plant out these trees. The ground was rock hard, and after managing to get only about a quarter of a metre into the soil we decided to fill the hole with water and hope that by soaking it we could penetrate the ground the next day.

Our precious fortnight was gradually disappearing. The room to the front of the cottage was still being used as our temporary lounge. Paul had tried to emulsion the ceiling on the previous visit. Our second attempt was more successful. We had brought with us two large tins of white emulsion paint, and after just one thick covering the ceiling looked great. I was then able to work on the windows which required re-puttying. Two cracked panes were replaced with glass we had had cut for us in England.

We had decided to put a picture rail around the room, approximately two feet down from the ceiling, counteracting its height of over nine feet and thus giving the illusion of a wider feel to the room. I then primed around the windows and continued to emulsion the walls with two coats of mellow sage, finally putting a white top coat on all woodwork.

In between painting the walls I worked on the small solid mahogany fireplace in the corner. It was sanded down to the original wood, then I used a stain to deepen the colour. I finally finished it off with two coats of satin varnish. A wrought-iron imitation log basket was placed in the hearth; an electric fire which could give us warmth on a chilly evening.

The two small easy chairs were returned into the room, along with an old solid wood bureau brought over on the trailer. Under the bureau compartment were three large drawers which would help with storage space. Either side of the bureau were two glass-fronted bookcases. One side we could use for books and in the other we stored the wine glasses. Eventually we would have cupboards in the kitchen. The room felt so different now; it was comforting to know that on future visits, when other rooms in the cottage were being worked on, we could retreat out of the upheaval to spend our evenings.

Only a few more days and our second visit would end. We reserved a table in a nearby restaurant to celebrate achievements so far. In the two trips to the cottage we had made only a small impression. Basically we had tidied up the rooms, and although having achieved an acceptable bathroom we knew a larger one was required. Also the newly-decorated room was only a temporary lounge, a stopgap to move our plans forward.

We decided that if the workmen returned with a realistic quotation for the staircase we would go ahead. On future holiday visits to the cottage it would be necessary to have the staircase in place, as it would set the layout for the ground floor, and with an entrance to the loft area we could get windows fitted, giving daylight to proceed with the work.

Luckily, the next day Denny turned up with Max, the French carpenter. They spent a couple of hours walking round the four rooms, trying to make a decision for the best entry point into the loft for the staircase. They came up with the idea of demolishing the wall between the existing kitchen and rear room with the red brick-built fireplace. This would open up the downstairs into one large room as you entered from the lobby.

The staircase would be across the open area, thereby dividing the room into two sections. The staircase would consist of ten steps, then divide from a centre platform into two side stairways, each with six steps. The idea was to get these side staircases either side of the iron rods in the loft area. They took all the measurements they needed to give us a final estimate for the work, which they could carry out after we had left. They were working on plans for installing windows in the loft, hoping to return on our last day with estimates.

They helped me to complete a complicated French form, which I returned to a small local post office to arrange to redirect any mail to our address in England. Gradually, as each French utility bill arrived, we made arrangements for it be paid by direct debit from our French bank account. If a bill was not paid on time you would get a ten percent increase on the charge when the reminder was sent, so it was very important not to have any post left in the *boîte aux lettres* outside the cottage. As we were only at the cottage twice a year for a two-week period, it was a long time for a letter to be answered or a bill unpaid.

On the north side of the cottage was the walkway from the front door round to the back. The ground was mostly covered in creeping ivy, growing out from under the tall overgrown privet hedge. The area just below the outlet pipes from the bathroom was buried under soil and we believed that this was where the fosse was concealed. The details of the property had described it possessed a *fosse septique*, but on talking to the garden men they explained that new laws would not permit a fosse to be so close to the well. We had received a hand-delivered notice from our Mairie (the office of the local Mayor at St Privat des Prés) that emptying waste water and surface water into the ditches would no longer be allowed. It seemed rural France was tightening up the laws and it would be necessary in the future to install a proper septic tank. The installation cost of one of these tanks would be in the region of £1,200. In view of the fact that we intended to build a bathroom on the other side of the property, where we had land that could accommodate the necessary pipes and drainage, the idea to go ahead seemed a practical solution. Denny said that existing toilet and wash-basin water from the small bathroom could be diverted into a sewer pipe which could run under the floorboards in the house and enter the tank along with the waste from the new bathroom. The installation would be undertaken by a local company specializing in these installations.

On clearing the ground just outside the small bathroom and removing the soil from around the waste pipes, I discovered the top of the opening trap to the fosse. It looked as if it had purposely been covered over with soil to disguise its existence. I wondered if what Denny had said about the fosse being near a well was the reason it had been deliberately hidden.

I then continued to hack at the surrounding undergrowth for about two hours and managed to make a small dent in the ivy covering the pathway. A very large laurel tree had a massive spread at the base and almost blocked off the access from the pathway to the back garden. It was about twenty feet high and screened off a great deal of light from the kitchen, its top branches touching the house. We had heard a noise each night around 4 am; a thud, then scampering across the ceiling above us while we were in bed. We believed some animal, possibly a pine marten or so we had been told, was jumping from the laurel tree through a large hole in the soffit to gain entry to the loft. Ray would wake me up each night and say, "It's there again, it's just scampered across the ceiling again, I wonder what it is?" I did not really care what it was, only that is was annoying to be woken up each night.

Using a tree saw, Ray removed several very large branches, which helped to improve the passageway. After that we did not hear the noise again. These heavy branches from the laurel tree were added to the other garden rubbish and were beginning to form a large heap for burning. We had been told by the garden men that bonfires are not allowed between May and September due to the risk of hot ash drifting onto the crops and starting fires. They agreed that if we left any rubbish they would burn it up on the last grass cut for the year.

At the front of the cottage were two trees which provided shade over the windows during the summer months. They were different from most trees and required an annual knuckle. The leaves grew on one-metre branches which were required to be cut back each autumn. I thought I would easily cut these branches off with the tree loppers in an hour, so one afternoon during the second week of our holiday I attempted this job. Two hours later I was still struggling, with aching arms. The next day Ray joined me and we tackled the job together, finally managing to strip the trees. A further dozen wheelbarrow loads of leafy branches were added to the pile of garden rubbish. It would appear that this would be a necessary garden chore each year.

Then we paid a visit to inspect the walnut trees at the bottom of our acre. Walking through the knee-high grass in our meadow, we wondered if it was due for cutting before winter. We knew from Denny that it had been cut in the spring after we left. Because the farmer could not get his tractor around the walnut trees, this meant the grass was now at waist height; it had dried out through the summer heat and was full of briars. An abundance of healthy-looking walnuts adorned the trees, not yet ready to drop. Unaware of what was involved in harvesting, because of the dense straw grass it seemed they would prove difficult to collect.

After cutting back the front trees we had an appointment at 4 pm with Ingrid and Terry for afternoon tea. As on my previous visit in the spring they were sitting in their garden surrounded by roses and other flowering shrubs. After introductions all round, they were keen to hear how we were progressing.

It was interesting to learn from them about all the inhabitants of our small hamlet. Ingrid and Terry had owned their cottage for the last twenty years and during this time had got to know the French inhabitants very well. Our neighbour Marie-Odette was referred by Ingrid as Madame Moyrand, so I considered myself honoured to be on first names with her. I explained that I had spoken to her in French and she had been very patient in understanding me. Ingrid told me that Madame Moyrand was fond of English cheddar cheese, having gained a liking for it while living in

England for a short time. The family had originated in Bordeaux but had retired to the village, where they owned various properties and surrounding land.

We were also told the names of the people in the hamlet along with their history and the pecking order of family importance. Ingrid and Terry's cottage was the end property and their large gardens backed onto the manor house round the corner at the end of the village. The gentleman who owned this house was a rich businessman who lived and conducted business in Bordeaux. Apparently he adored staying at his country home most weekends, accompanied by his wife. He had a live-in caretaker who attended to all the garden maintenance, including the pond, while he was away.

We enquired as to why a cottage in the village had the number 74 on the front. They knew the house had once been connected to the railway, having been built and owned by the French railway network. In fact the railway line had actually passed through the hamlet. They did not know the origin of the number.

We were then invited to take a tour of their extensive garden, which was divided into several areas. Each section had been worked as a different project over the years. Their main hobby in France was the garden, which was evident from the amount of loving care which had been devoted to it. They had a large circle of friends with whom they socialized, including many French acquaintances. They both spoke French, not fluently but enough to get by on, which was more than we could possibly manage at present.

They were a lovely couple and had made us feel at home

in the hamlet, especially now that we had some first-hand knowledge of our French neighbours. They were staying until late October, but hopefully they would see us again next May when we returned.

Finally, after several digging attempts, we managed to plant our apple trees, along with secure stakes to support them against the strong winds that sometimes blow up just before a heavy Dordogne thunderstorm. We had been told about these sudden and violent storms but had yet to experience one.

On our last full day at the cottage, while packing the trailer for the return journey, Denny and Danny turned up with Max the carpenter. They had a printed quotation with a realistic price for a bespoke staircase finished in solid pine. Their enquiries regarding dormer windows had revealed that planning permission would be required before going ahead with this work. According to building regulations they would have to match our neighbour's property. Building dormer windows in stone to comply with these conditions would prove costly. They suggested that if we were to consider Velux windows, no planning permission would be required.

They quoted us a price for four windows, two large ones and two smaller ones. The large windows would be placed in the rooms at each end of the loft. The area over the top of the stairway and the open area would have the two small ones. This all sounded good to us, even though, as yet, we did not know which end of the loft would be a bathroom and which a bedroom. Included in the price was the work involved in dismantling the wall between the two rooms. They expected to install the staircase within the next two months.

Before they left, they enquired as to whether our house had been connected to the railway. They said it was so well constructed that they believed it to have been built as a railway property. This was intriguing, as we had found evidence of railway conductors around the garden along with an old sleeper joint.

Thankful to think that work could begin to get the basics in place, we paid our deposit, giving them the key to start the work after we left. They promised it would be finished by mid-November. Then we decided it would be a good idea to return after completion and take all necessary measurements for the new kitchen area. On our next visit in May we would bring a flatpack kitchen in the trailer.

Before leaving the cottage we decided it would be prudent to make sure everything was securely packed away against the winter weather. On local advice the water was turned off at the stop-cock and the pipes drained down. The mattress was covered in plastic and all the pillows and blankets well wrapped and stored in a small built-in corner cupboard in the newly decorated temporary lounge. Again I left the mouse powders around and covered our chairs sealing the cushions in black plastic. Other odd furniture was covered with dust sheets.

We returned to England and made arrangements to return during November to inspect the new staircase. Denny had promised photos when the staircase was in situ and assured us that the windows were on order and would be installed shortly.

In October, shortly after our return, Ray received some

disturbing news from the company he had been employed by for the past ten years; the future of his job was in doubt.

In his late forties Ray had become disillusioned with his trade as a television engineer. The rental companies were losing customers because of the reliability of the newer-style televisions. His employer had centralised the reporting depot, forcing their employees to drive long distances and requiring the engineers to repair a set work allocation each day. This pressure was forcing a lot of television engineers to seek other professions.

An opportunity had arisen for him to obtain a temporary six-month position with a London-based company which was responsible for monitoring television viewing audiences, with a possibility of a permanent position if the company successfully gained the new contract. Initially Ray covered the Swindon and South West area, but a year later it became a permanent job. Over the years he had found it a very interesting company to work, for far less stressful than trying to keep up the pressure of repairing ten to twelve televisions a day.

This company where he had been so happy working for the last ten years was now advising him that they had been unsuccessful in obtaining the latest four-year contract. This meant that the following year they would be making redundancies on quite a large scale. Next year Ray would have reached the age of fifty-nine. He had already decided to take early retirement at sixty-one to coincide with my retirement at sixty, but it now seemed his working career might fall short of this target. The position would not become clear, however, until next spring.

It would not be a good idea to sleep at the cottage when we returned in November. Without central heating and all the bedding packed away it was more practical to stay in a hotel. Our favourite corner café in Aubeterre had rooms on the third and fourth floors and this would be a good spot; we could easily reach our cottage during the day. We booked the ferry crossing and made a reservation with the hotel.

Arriving in November, we were surprised how many people were in the café in the middle of winter. It was a chilly evening, but the log-burning stove was roaring and we sat by the welcome heat and enjoyed our meal. We were looking forward to seeing the new staircase tomorrow. Although we had received digital photos, we were very much looking forward to a close inspection of the work and the new layout of the room, and the men were due on site sometime during the day.

Arriving on a chilly November morning, the cottage did not feel damp. We had bought some groceries to keep ourselves fed during the day and make drinks using bottled water. The staircase was impressive as we entered from the lobby doorway. The wall between the two rooms had been demolished and cleared away. The old door and frame had been saved for future use in the loft area.

The new stairway, finished in light untreated pine, looked very dominant. It rose from the centre of the now singular room. It divided half way up in two sections - one to the left and one to the right, each flight of steps ending into a dark gaping hole in the ceiling. Sadly there was no evidence of daylight through new windows. No work on the windows had started.

We climbed the stairs and shone a torch into the dark void. The iron rods were still a problem. Although the left side of the staircase got us behind the rods, on the opposite side access across the loft was still blocked by them. The idea of a dividing staircase had not really worked. Where the ceiling had been cut away for the staircase entry, the ends of the supporting beams were suspended by chains from the roof rafters.

We now viewed the new downstairs layout, with a view to planning the new rooms. Entry from the lobby was now into one large room but the staircase seemed to dominate and divide the room quite starkly.

After our initial surprise at the intrusive look of the staircase we realised that this new layout favoured us having the dining area at the end of the room which was at present the old kitchen. We would be able to use the existing chimney exits in the corner to site a log-burning stove, making a focal point. The other side of the staircase could be the area for the new kitchen. It certainly would be more practical, as there was a doorway leading to the room we were now using as our bedroom. Once we had a new bedroom in the loft, this room could become the new lounge. It would be perfect, because in the long flat back wall we could have an opening. This new doorway would lead directly into the back garden. Food from the new kitchen could easily be carried through the top corner of the lounge to a designed eating area, saving the long trudge from the front door.

At last, after months of drawing sketches and designing a plan for the ground floor, the solution was now beginning to emerge. The basic framework was now coming together, but it would be several years before completion. Before building a backdoor we first had to build a new bedroom, bathroom and landing area.

Then there was a knock on the front door. Denny and Danny had turned up to see what we thought of the alterations. The older man, Denny, was limping badly. It turned out he had recently had a bad fall and had ended up in hospital receiving a hip replacement; hence the reason no windows had been installed.

We talked about our first impressions of the staircase and the plans for the rooms. They assured us that they would get the windows started as soon as they could; also they had a plan for the removal of the iron rods. By incorporating heavy timber supports these would take the weight of the existing roof beams. As we would not be back at the cottage until next May they assured us they had plenty of time to implement the work before our return.

After they left we continued to take accurate measurements in the area that would now become the new kitchen. The small red-brick fireplace would have to be dismantled to make way for the corner sink unit. We decided on a straight run of units and work-surface along the back wall, siting our new oven in the centre and returning units round the other corner ending with the free standing fridge-freezer.

As the staircase had been finished in untreated natural pine it looked very dominant. Obviously it had to have further work to protect the raw wood. We decided to bring over a dark oak wood stain. Darkening the staircase would make it blend in better with the room.

Once we had the necessary sizes to draw up plans for our kitchen, we returned to the hotel for the night. Tomorrow we were returning to England. During the long winter months we would have plenty of time to plan and purchase a kitchen.

Exploration and excavation

Keeping to our budget, we sought a reasonably-priced kitchen, deciding upon antique mellow pine units with contrasting light beige work-surfaces. As it was quite dark up that end of the room, anything that reflected light would be an advantage. Although there was a large window, it was on the north side and did not let in sunlight.

The kitchen arrived direct from the warehouse; after inspection we found that two of the carcasses were split and would have to be returned, along with doors intended for different units. On replacement we carefully checked each item, as once out in France there was no way of exchanging the equipment. Satisfied we had the correct parts, we were able to start packing.

Unfortunately the weight of the carcasses, drawers, doors and two three metre lengths of worktop, plus a five-litre can of dark oak wood stain for staining the staircase, was going to create a lot of strain on the trailer along with all the work tools. A lot of thought went into deciding the best way to load.

The ceiling of the intended kitchen area consisted of old-fashioned polystyrene tiles which were brown in colour and peeling off. These would be discarded. So our plan for the two weeks was to remove this ceiling and the small brick-built corner fireplace. If the men had made headway in the loft installing new windows this area could now be cleaned, as there would now be daylight. Ray intended to paper the bathroom walls with blown vinyl paper to improve the finish. I intended to decorate the lobby.

Since Ray had learned in early March that his firm's contract had not been renewed, he had found that he could put in for a redundancy package at the end of May. It was a blow to our plans, as our finances were geared around his retiring at sixty-one. Luckily our cottage was not dependent on expensive restoration materials or professional help, the labour side being undertaken by Ray, which was the object of our early retirement plans. Also the budget for renovation materials was in position. As Ray would not be drawing his state pension until he was sixty-five, we would be relying on a pension maturing from his fifteen years' service in the television trade which had been frozen and matured when he was sixty.

The package offered by his company was a lump sum, based on basic compensation payments, not huge by any means. But included was the opportunity to purchase his two-year-old Peugeot 406 at a realistic price. This would solve our transport requirements, as during his career we had relied on him having a company car. The lump sum would help to cover our daily expenses for the rest of the eighteen months until I retired.

So in early June and with Ray now free from the employment rat-race, we set off on the usual route. If I had been concerned before about pulling an overloaded trailer, this time was even more stressful. I sat with fingers tightly crossed as we pulled out of the Limpley Stoke valley. That part went OK, but when we got to the ferry terminal we had to pull up a very steep wet ramp. Just at the brow an official in uniform held their hand up to stop. I just waved my arms at him and Ray kept going. Luckily at the last minute he realised the problem and stepped aside. If we had stopped I dread to imagine the consequences of trying to pull away on a very steep and slippery ramp.

Every pull across to France seemed to be getting worse. Each time I vowed we would not pull another heavy load, as it was not worth the anxiety through the journey. But still we carried on, filling our trailer to the maximum possible limit time and time again.

As we pulled onto the driveway we could see that the two large windows had been installed in the loft. I knew straight away they had been put in the wrong place.

There were large piles of soil to one side of the tracks and a gaping hole in the side of the cottage leading underground. A pipe came out from under the foundations, leading into a new half-covered septic tank. All around were deep muddy weals in the grass caused by a heavy vehicle, probably a tractor. We entered the cottage and started to open up after the long winter months.

On surveying the work in the loft we confirmed that the two large windows had been placed too high up in the roof; when standing by them it was not possible to see out. Obviously by inserting a window higher into the slope of the roof you get maximum light, but we had wanted the windows lower so we could see the countryside from the new rooms.

Within an hour Denny had turned up to explain about the mess in the garden. The company undertaking the work had been brought to a halt by very wet weather. To continue would have only caused further damage to the surrounding area. They would return to complete the job when the ground was drier. The septic tank had been successfully installed, although no pipes from the house had yet been connected.

When we told him we were not happy about the windows, he assured us it could be remedied and the windows cut into the roof lower down. Max the carpenter had decided to go nearer the apex to gain more overhead light. They were due to return after our visit to install the two small ones, so they would be refitted then.

It was disappointing to have found the outside of the cottage in such a mess. Because of the wet weather the grass had not been cut and was beginning to get out of hand again. We hoped that Denny would be true to his word and turn up soon and get it tidy.

The loft situation was a concern because they had not managed to remove the iron rods and we only had their promise it was going to happen. Still as we have found out over successive visits, things do not go to plan when you are undertaking restorations and renovations. Especially when the work is out of your hands; timescales and promises are rarely to schedule.

We did the usual routine; although we uncoupled the trailer from the car it was not until Saturday that we could unpack all the new kitchen flatpacks to store in the workshop. Ray began wallpapering the bathroom. It seemed to me that we were never going to move forward; we were still doing work in that small room. I took advantage of the fact that we now had daylight in the loft by making a start on removing all the dirt and debris from the area.

Between the rafters and all along the walls were great thick bundles of cobwebs which had accumulated over the years, never having seen the light of day. I am the worst coward when it comes to spiders, so the thought of cobwebs did not really appeal. Nevertheless, I was determined to overcome my squeamishness and make a positive start. I covered myself in a strong green cotton boiler suit and tucked all my hair under protective headgear; the thought of any spiders dropping down on me was abhorrent. With rubber gloves as protection I started at the end by the loft hatch. I used an ordinary floor broom, brushing down between the rafters. Black dirt from under the roof tiles, along with dust and webs, dropped to the floor as I worked my way along the loft.

After three hours I had worked along approximately a third of the area. I kept stopping to sweep the piles of rubbish into black bags. It was definitely a great improvement. As I continued along each side I was aware that I was not finding any recent cobwebs and very little evidence of spiders. I began to get more confident in attacking the old webs. On reaching the really dark and hidden areas, where I had to crawl under beams to reach the dirt, I felt less inhibited about finding spiders. However, I did find plenty of mouse skeletons in the corners and on the side ledges.

I continued with this mammoth task throughout the whole of the next day, finally taking up the vacuum cleaner to finish the job. It certainly had made a tremendous difference. We could now look up through the hole in the ceiling at the top of the staircase into daylight without wondering what was scurrying around up there.

Now it was clean enough to spend a few hours taking measurements to get an idea of the space available in which to design the new rooms. In order to cover the whole loft with a new ceiling, the space between the rafters would first have to be insulated, then plasterboard fixed to them. The main central timber beam running the length of the cottage and the two lower beams either side were not going to be covered. Along the side were two heavy support beams, with the iron rods protruding across the loft to the duplicate support beams opposite. These heavy supports would lend themselves to being boxed in to start forming the partitions across the loft, thus splitting the whole area into three sections.

The slope of the roof went right down to the floorboards on either side, so it would be practical for a thick insulated stud partition to form the inside wall, this to be placed one metre in from the sides. This would keep a sensible head height towards the edge.

The new bedroom would be best sited at the far end (which was actually to the front of the cottage). The window would give a view to the south side. The approximate size of the room would be three metres wide by seven metres in length.

At the top of the left-hand staircase the area would be best left open. Then you would turn right along a small hallway. This would run along the front of the new bathroom, leading down to the bedroom. To get full head height in the bathroom and allow for a shower, the room would have to be built close to the centre of the loft space. We decided that Max, by putting the bathroom window high up, had achieved the correct position. We would ask that only the bedroom window be moved to a lower position.

This left a central area of three square metres where a small window was going to be fitted. This could be an open mezzanine area, the side of which would be finished off with balustrades and a handrail for protection around the stairway. We then realised, much to our delight and amazement, that we were going to have very thick beams, exposed against a backdrop of white ceiling. At the moment they were hairy, woodwormed and a dirty medium oak colour, but after sanding, distressing, staining dark oak and varnishing we would have ourselves some very choice exposed beams. Character after all!

Now we had cleared the area, the next project was to replace the temporary chains in the loft; these supported the cut-off beams which finished in mid-air over the new staircase opening. Ray intended to replace each chain with a wooden support. Making good progress, I was assisting him, standing on a beam being supported by a chain.

Suddenly his eyes opened wide, an expression of fear on his face. He shouted at me, "Don't move, whatever you do, don't move!" Believing something horrid was about to drop onto me, I froze. But it wasn't that. "A link is broken in the chain, could go any minute, stand completely still" hissed Ray.

I looked at the chain and he was right, one link was wide open. I stared transfixed at the gap but it did not appear to be opening any further. I stood perfectly still. It did not seem to widen so I stepped back, edging my way across the beam so my weight was now resting on the next one. I was rather relieved I had not come down with the beam into the kitchen below. I could see the danger if my weight had been enough to snap the chain, but I did think he had overreacted a little. I put it down to him being a bit up tight after the events that morning.

As we did the weekly shop in Ribérac it had been hammering down with rain, so we had parked the car near the shop entrance. Usually we avoid parking close to other cars as French motorists are not careful when they open their car doors, and most of their cars have dents from doors swinging open. However we were unlucky this time. On returning to our car after the shop we could see that the right wing and bumper had been smashed in by some careless driver, either reversing badly or swinging in far too close.

Ray was livid. "I don't believe it!" he fumed. "We never park close to people. The one time I do, this happens."

The car was badly damaged. The offside wing and bumper would have to be replaced and the side sprayed. There was no sign of another car with damage or a note under the windscreen. We will never know the culprit, who had obviously disappeared very quickly, leaving us to sort out the repair with the insurance company on our newly-acquired car when we returned to England. C'est la vie!

Although our plan was to install the new kitchen on our autumn visit, we now knew it would not be possible to undertake a full rewire until we were retired. Ray had been checking through a forum of ex-pats on the internet, and had found that French wiring is completely different to the English system.

After finishing papering out the downstairs bathroom, the next task was to remove the red brick fireplace from the corner. It was a shame - we were trying to keep original features - but it had to go because we needed to fit the sink in this corner. It was difficult to dismantle and was taken out brick by brick. The remains of the hearth area were made level with a compound and an air brick inserted to keep the flow of air through the old chimney up to the stack.

Ray began removing the ceiling tiles. These had been glued on with four blobs to each tile and the glue was resistant to any attempt at removal from the plasterboard. The ceiling surface now looked in a terrible mess, and we decided the best way out of the situation was to cover up the unevenness with textured paint. If applied fairly thick it would disguise the glue blobs and we could create a stipple finish before a coat of white emulsion. We would bring this special paint on the next visit.

Denny and Danny returned at the weekend to start grass cutting. It took them a long time and they had to resort to using the strimmer in some areas. They assured us that they would continue with the work upstairs after we had returned to England; we explained our plans for the new bathroom area and requested that only the bedroom window was lowered. Denny said he would chase up the firm to finish the septic tank installation, which included laying a new driveway from our entrance up to the old barn where we kept the car. They had given us a good price to carry out this work as they could use the heavy digging equipment while the men were working on the tank installation which required long trenches out into our acre.

Our friends Judy and Brian were staying at their cottage, so on the Saturday evening they paid us a visit to see the progress we had made so far. They approved of the staircase installation and agreed it had been worth getting it done, as it would open up the rooms for future expansion. Listening to our plans for the eventual layout, they thought a new doorway to the garden would improve things immensely.

We then introduced them to the restaurant where we had enjoyed a meal when our son stayed. This was on a quiet back road that we used to reach their cottage. We arranged a return visit the following week to see all their improvements.

It was the start of our second week; I continued to work in the small lobby area. The wallpaper was soon removed, as it was already separating from the wall through old age. I undercoated and painted round the front door and new panelling under the bevelled glass insert. I put emulsion on the walls and scrubbed up the original ceramic floor tiles. It certainly was an improvement as you entered the house.

During our second week we decided to have a day out in the town of Périgueux, the capital city of the Dordogne region. So far we had enjoyed beautiful sunny weather throughout our stay and that day followed the same pattern. The route was through rolling countryside with many fields full of the beautiful bright yellow colza. We journeyed on traffic-free main roads. Everywhere looked green and refreshed; trees were leafing after the winter months and buds bursting into flower on fruit trees. As we approached Périgueux we dropped down into the valley in which it lies. On one side of road were the high cliffs of the gorge covered with large magnificent trees, on our right the river Isle.

On the outskirts of the main town were the usual trading estates that house the large malls and specialist stores for the masses. We now often visit these shops to obtain purchases of large items; they have an excellent choice and are great value. Continuing towards Périgueux, we drove through the busy streets leading into the centre. Luckily we ended up opposite a large underground car park. Leaving the car park we found ourselves in the centre of the main shops, which were very impressive. Along the sides of the main highway the Wednesday market was in full swing. We turned off into a pedestrian only area. Winding our way through the narrow streets we entered a large square surrounded by small cafés and restaurants. The tables and chairs were gradually being arranged outside each café and we joined other people sitting in the sunshine for a morning coffee.

We then explored the different alleyways that led into this beautiful central area. The buildings were very old indeed; we wandered around the small specialist shops admiring the quality of the items for sale. Chocolate shops I had never seen the like of in England presented the most temptingly-wrapped chocolates. Expensive jewellery shops displayed exquisite combinations of precious stones. Boutiques tucked into corners offered outrageous outfits in leather. The specialist knife and gun shops provided a magnificent choice of equipment, probably aimed at the local hunting community. The designer clothing shops seemed to be in the main high street exhibiting chic fashions and colours that were the latest in *haute couture* for the coming summer.

The maze of narrow streets eventually led us to an exit by the large cathedral of Périgueux. Some seats were available at the rear of this impressive building in a quiet shady area under large leafy trees. We took time to relax surrounded by the rampart walls which overlook the river running through the city. We then retraced our steps back through the small streets until we again found the main central square.

By now the tables were filling up quickly as it was lunchtime. We wandered round the square checking out the menus on offer from at least a dozen restaurants and deciding on the most tempting. We sat under the shade of a large canopy enjoying our lunch and wine. In the afternoon we walked around the main high street shops and purchased some items. What an enjoyable day; the old town itself was quite magical, hidden away in deep thick stone walls waiting to be found and explored.

To finish our day we had been invited to Judy and Brian's for supper, and their cottage was easily reached on our return journey. We enthused about our trip to Périgueux and the luxury of having a day off from working on our property. We could see that they had made some further improvements since our last visit. There was a new roof, which had been an expensive undertaking; their cottage covered a large area, having the lounge and three bedrooms on ground level. The roof had been leaking in several places and temporary repairs were not holding in heavy downpours. It had been done in two stages and the second stage was nearing completion. Like us they had no felt under the roof tiles and this had now been fitted. The roofers had inserted two Velux windows in the ceiling of the very high lounge, greatly increasing the amount of daylight in the room. The roof felt was exposed between the rafters, but their plan was to insulate between the beams with glass fibre and create a ceiling with plasterboard. They showed us where they had started this work on their mezzanine area. It had certainly made a difference and the white plasterboard made the area cosy.

Their mezzanine loft area stretched over the three bedrooms so it was very large, albeit very low at the sides where the roof sloped away to floor level (much like our loft at present). In the centre the height was just about ample enough to walk around as long as you ducked under the supporting beams. Their next plan was to divide the area at the highest point with a partition, thus creating a large sloping bedroom one side and an en suite the other.

The tall barn adjoining their cottage had an earth floor which they intended to concrete over in stages. This would enable them to leave a car permanently in France, the intention being to fly rather than have the long drive from either the Caen or St Malo ferryports. There was a possibility of a new air route opening up at Bergerac airport, only one hour's drive away, with flights connecting to our local airport at Bristol. Also a plan was under way for a swimming pool during the following year. Although not having as much ground surrounding their cottage as us, there was enough to accommodate a large pool and patio area for sunbathing. The evening passed quickly as we chatted about future plans, and we parted with a promise to meet up again in England.

During the remainder of our stay we removed a dysfunctional extractor hood from the old kitchen area. It consisted of imitation wood cladding and was positioned over the now extinct cooker. This ugly-looking piece was about one and half metres down from the ceiling. At ceiling level it had expelled steam to an external chimney. The flue for this was contained in a thick brick stack built three metres high in the loft area finishing out on the roof and capped with a couple of tin pot chimney pots.

When the extractor hood was ripped from the wall it revealed a damp area where water had been seeping from the roof. Ray decided that next autumn he would have to find where the leak was coming from and get it repaired. This extractor would not have worked, as it was completely stuffed up with a bird's nest and other rubbish. I could now remove the final traces of the old wallpaper; although we still had bare walls and scruffy paintwork, it had all been washed down. With the whole room opened up it was now a fairly large area to move around in. On our next visit we could start work on installing the new kitchen units at the opposite end.

The neighbour opposite, Madame Moyrand, received the bi-annual visit from her relatives and we were invited for apéritifs, being introduced to Sophie, who was the wife of Marie-Odette's brother Philip. Sophie had arrived in France at the age of 18 to *travailler au pair*. She had quickly learned to speak the French language and explained the easiest way was to be thrown in the deep end. She had lived and worked in Paris and eventually met and married Philip; they now lived in Normandy. It was great to chat with them as Sophie was interpreting our questions about the village. Marie-Odette had retired to her property with her husband from Bordeaux. Their property had large gardens, orchards and rights to some of the surrounding woodland and fields around the hamlet which were rented out to the farmer for cultivation.

We told them our plans for retirement and said we were hoping to spend more time in France, to put the property in better shape and eventually build rooms upstairs. I think it put Marie-Odette's mind at rest that we did not intend to rent it out to various people during the summer months. It was a nice feeling to know we had started to make friends with the

French. Sophie explained to us that the inhabitants of the village will leave you alone if you don't speak with them; they think you don't want to get involved. If you make an effort they will be happy to welcome you and converse back.

On departing, Ray, trying out his French, tried to say we were having fish for dinner tonight. "Le pèche est dans la cuisine" he said. With that our hosts went into fits of laughter. Sophie explained he had said we were "fishing in the kitchen". So much for starting to make an effort with our French.

We returned to England for the summer months and began to plan our next visit. It was now early September 2001 and we had managed to arrange our stay for three weeks. On this visit we had our daughter Caroline accompanying us. She was keen to see the cottage; it was her first visit and she knew about all the work we had embarked on. To our amazement the new motorway link was now open, and instead of the tiresome journey through Niort we could bypass this town by staying on the new section of road. It was great, as it cut the journey time down a lot, and once we had turned off at the Pons junction we completed the last few miles in the early evening sunshine.

As we turned into the new driveway our hearts began to beat a little faster. It looked so good; a wide drive finished in white compacted stones running right up to the old barn with a neat turning area adjacent to the drive. It was unbelievable the difference it made. The new *fosse septique* had been covered up and the whole area looked flat and tidy. The builders had resited the bedroom window in the right place and put in the other two smaller windows. Inside, above the ascending staircase was a window letting in daylight. The iron rods were no longer blocking the walkway; there was evidence of very strong supporting beams replacing the rods. As agreed the bathroom window had been left in the original place, giving maximum light. The newly resited bedroom window was great; now we could look over the surrounding countryside. The small window opposite the one over the stairs let in daylight for the open-plan area.

We noticed too that the original loft hatch entry had been removed and Max had put in a proper window frame and made an opening window. Now we could look out over the white winding lane disappearing in the distance. With the provision of all these windows the whole area was bright and airy. Our daughter had seen the early pictures of the cottage and could appreciate the improvements that had been carried out. Even so she expressed her surprised at how much work was still to be undertaken. We then set off to the usual spot in Aubeterre for a good meal of long-awaited French cooking.

The next day was the usual trip into Ribérac, taking Caroline to experience the market and returning with all the provisions for the coming week. The afternoon was spent unpacking the trailer. This time we had managed to bring over a solid antique pine Welsh dresser along with an oval pine dining table. These had been well packed and covered for protection in bubble and were placed in the cycle shed. We decided they would not be unwrapped until we had finished decorating the dining room end. No point in keep moving furniture all around the place; as long we had managed to get it over it would keep for the future. Still to be brought across on the trailer was a second-hand three piece cottage suite, which would eventually be for the new lounge.

On Saturday I introduced Caroline to Marie-Odette and explained that she was with us for few days' holiday. The following Thursday we would take her to Angoulême to catch the TGV back to Paris. She was going to have the last few days of her holiday visiting places in Paris before catching a plane from Charles de Gaulle airport to Bristol.

In the afternoon we worked in the garden, hacking back the overgrowth from the summer. Where soil had been returned over the new septic tank and other exposed areas, weeds had quickly grown. After digging and levelling the earth we spread grass seed into the bald patches. On inspection the three new apple trees looked healthy and seemed to have survived their first year.

On the Sunday we decided to have a trip out to a nearby beauty spot called La Jemaye. It was a natural beauty spot surrounding a *grand étang* (large lake). We took a picnic in the cooler box. On arriving we were far from alone, as many French families had also come for a day by the lake. Along one side of the water tons of sand had been spread, forming a man-made beach. Quite a few people were sunbathing, others swimming in the lake. There were diving boards placed in the deeper water, where adventurous divers were showing off their skills. Modern shower huts were provided. A large indoor restaurant served lunches which extended onto a patio area with shaded tables.

We drove round to the other side of the lake, where there was plenty of parking under shady trees. Scattered around were permanent tables and adjoining benches for the visitors to enjoy their picnics. Needless to say many were occupied, the families having spread a tablecloth and set out crockery. Fresh baguettes were being cut at the table and wine was being served from coolers.

Among the trees were various marked footpaths leading through many acres of forest. We followed one trail for a kilometre and found ourselves at a bird-hide in a remote part of the woodlands area adjacent to the lake. Inside the hut there was comfortable seating for watching wildlife that might be spotted, with pictures and drawings of the common species for children to recognize. After our stroll we settled down in the shade for our picnic and enjoyed the rest of the afternoon in the pleasant surroundings.

There are three other natural park areas, with a man-made beach surrounding a lake or river, within an easy drive from our cottage. They are completely free to enter, kept immaculately clean and maintained for the enjoyment of the French people. These areas are found all over France. It is a legacy the French expect of their country.

The next day Caroline got to work in the bathroom, having offered to emulsion the newly-papered walls. Ray proceeded to check out the leak in the old kitchen area. He had discovered that some lead flashing was missing round the base of the chimney and at the same time wanted to inspect the outlets on the chimney stack.

First he had to assemble the ladder. He used the rope and

pulley to extend the dual ladder to its full height. Attached was a gadget that hooked over one of the rungs to lock the two ladders together. Being extra cautious, Ray had tied the top of the ladder to the gutter area in case the ladder slipped sideways. He was always aware that it was better to err on the side of safety; we did not want to have an accident that would mean a hospital visit and incur medical charges. Any ladder work usually entailed me standing on the bottom rung as a precaution. But today he felt happy that he had secured the ladder safely.

A little later I passed by, shouting up to him, "You OK up there?" Ray turned, and as he did so the ladder pulled sideways. Because it was fixed at the top, the hook came off the rung and the bottom part of the ladder started to slip away. I pushed against the bottom and tried to get the hook to re-clip, but it was not possible. I shouted out to Caroline, hoping she would hear. Meanwhile Ray was clinging to the ladder.

"Whatever you do, don't move about" I said.

"Don't worry, just get the hook back on" he replied.

Easier said than done, I thought, with Ray stuck twenty feet up a ladder which was coming apart in the middle. Caroline heard my frantic cry for assistance and came running from the bathroom area. After assessing the situation she rushed off to get the stepladder. Luckily, between us, me pushing upwards and her on the steps negotiating the hook, we were able to realign it. It was a good job our daughter was staying. Afterwards Ray replaced the hook idea with his own invention to secure the two ladders together. I suppose if he hadn't tied the ladder at the top it wouldn't have occurred, a case of being too over-cautious.

From inspecting the top of the tall stack he could see that there were three separate extracts leading from the kitchen; only two were covered by individual pots. Evidently the middle one was open; it was feasible we were getting rain down this flue. He decided to discard these old tin pots, cover two of the extracts leaving one open for future use and get one proper chimney stack. He took all the measurements for us to bring one next time.

On Tuesday 11th September 2001 we took Caroline into Périgueux, as we felt we must show her the delights of the old town. We returned home for early evening and as we were preparing our meal our son Paul telephoned to impart the terrible tragic events of the day in America. Not being in touch with a radio or a television, it was hard for us to comprehend what had occurred. It was not until we returned to England, and saw it visually, that we could begin to realise the magnitude of what had happened on that day, and how it was going to change history forever.

The following day Caroline put on a second coat of emulsion, which completed the bathroom. At long last the room was finished. Or so we thought.

Ray started to put the special textured paint onto the ceiling in the new kitchen area to cover up the rough plasterboard. Everywhere was covered up with dust sheets, including the new staircase; he was using a roller and it flicked off in all directions. It was a terrible job and covered everywhere in large blobs of thick splashes as he formed a stipple effect, but finally he had covered the whole area. Cleaning up took absolutely ages, but we all agreed it had created a good ceiling and just needed a coat of white emulsion for a perfect finish.

I said, "I am not looking forward to you having to repeat that messy job up the new dining room end, but I know you must." Ray replied, "You might not. I've had an idea about creating exposed beams. If we take down the whole ceiling, polystyrene tiles and plasterboard, we will be left with the supporting beams showing. Like upstairs, they will need sanding and distressing to make them look old. Then we'll put new plasterboard in between and finish off with the dark oak stain that we're using on the staircase. We'll then have exposed beams downstairs as well as upstairs."

"Great" I said. I knew our little cottage had potential; it just needed discovering.

It had been a warm day outside and it was great to enjoy our meal in the garden to get some fresh air. Afterwards we decided to explore the walk called 'Le Grand Tour'. Leaving the front gate, we turned right down the white lane, passing our boundary of the overgrown privet hedge for approximately forty metres and finishing at the back of our barn with laurel and lilac trees. The deep ditch skirted along the side of our acre up to the far edge of our property with the walnut trees. Opposite was a field of cattle belonging to the beef farmer. The white lane gradually climbed for about a third of a mile. At the top it curved round to the right with the edge of a deep copse on your left. This too belonged to the farmer, who owned the rights to cut the trees for logs. Notices saying 'private' kept us out of the wood.

The lane continued past twenty rows of vines either side and more open crop growing fields, plus a very large hay shed containing numerous bales of hay. Each morning the son of Monsieur Sautet drove his tractor up the white lane and returned with two bales. Up to then I had no idea how much hay cows consume. Believe me it's enormous; his daily trip continued throughout the summer months, even when the cows were grazing.

Continuing on along the lane, copse one side and crops the other, we came to another white lane running across; a T junction. Now a choice - left or right. We turned left and then walked for twenty minutes towards a small hamlet tucked away in a small corner with a mixture of stone properties and a pretty bread oven covered in hanging baskets. This led out to a road on the outskirts of our hamlet. It was a complete circle of about two kilometres, taking about fifty minutes to walk at a leisurely pace.

The next day we took Caroline to Angoulême to catch the fast train to Paris. She had enjoyed her visit, seeing the surrounding area and towns near the cottage and said she hoped to return soon when, hopefully, we would have made further progress.

Using a hand-held belt-sander, Ray began removing the top layer of dirt from the floorboards in the new kitchen area and under the staircase. It was a very slow process and took a lot of energy, but the results looked encouraging and we began to see light, clean pine floorboards.

A picture rail was fixed around this area, as we had done in the temporary lounge. We would put the tall kitchen wall cupboards up to the height of the rail. This meant they would be fairly high, but as the ceiling was so tall it was better to balance them out. He then re-puttied the window panes on the tall windows, renewing panes that were beyond saving. The new textured ceiling and surrounding walls received two coats of emulsion down to the new picture rail. Ray could now start positioning and fixing wall cupboards.

I was kept busy hand-sanding the wood of the new staircase. Once it was smooth and free of rough areas, the dust was washed off. I could then apply the first coat of dark oak stain. This was a full day's work, as there was a lot of wood to cover.

The following day I started the second coat, until I achieved the depth of colour that looked just right. We had come to an important decision. Although we had this splendid staircase that divided in two half way up, only the left-hand side was necessary. As the iron rods had now successfully been removed, it seemed unnecessary to have two entries to the loft; the stairway took up value space. Ray suggested that if he removed these extra steps we could reinstate the ceiling beams and win back floor space upstairs.

It was the second weekend of our visit and we were grateful to not have to pack up and go home; we had another whole week left. There still might be a chance of getting the kitchen units out of their packaging and assembled. I spent the next two days painting two coats of varnish sealer over the dark oak stain on the staircase in the mornings, then assembling kitchen units and cupboards in the afternoons. The cardboard packaging from the units was saved and stored in the cycle shed.

Ray had carefully worked out the measurements for the base units; they would all line up exactly under the wall cupboards. A space was left for the oven (which we were still using up the other end of the kitchen along with the sink). This would be central to the units, with an extractor hood slotting between the wall cupboards. Although we had taken our measurements carefully, we knew from previous attempts at installing kitchen units there was no guarantee it all would line up.

Where we had removed the fireplace in this room it left a squared-off corner. The floor units were positioned along the back wall, finishing short of the corner. A double sink unit was placed adjacent to the floor units, finishing at the edge of the window. Worktops would be cut to fit over all the units, including a specially-cut triangle piece to fit the corner.

Luckily the units fitted according to plan and we made good progress during the early part of the week. The handles, pelmets and cornicing were fitted and work could then begin on cutting in the worktops. These were cut outside, making life a lot easier; after the necessary jointing with bolts it was all beginning to take shape. We decided the sink would be cut into the worktop on the next visit.

In Ribérac we purchased two sheets of hardboard to cover the floorboards a metre wide in front of the units; we tiled over the hardboard with plastic tiles, making it practical and washable for everyday wear. While Ray laid the new floor tiles I put four rows of tiles above the worktops on the kitchen walls.

While in Ribérac we noticed a large display of log-burning stoves. We took time to check these out, taking measurements and information available on small stoves. Several were on special offer and one in particular looked perfect for the corner of our dining room. We decided to return with our trailer to purchase it. It was placed on the trailer by a fork-lift truck. Unfortunately on returning to the cottage it was not so easy to remove. After unpacking we virtually had to dismantle it before we could lift it off the trailer. Eventually it was rebuilt and stored in the corner of the workshop, covered for protection as installation would not be for another two years.

On this visit we were staying a week later into the month, so we were able to collect some of our walnuts. We managed to flatten a lot of the straw-like grass surrounding our trees and spread a plastic sheet. By knocking off the nuts with a long pole, the ones that were ready fell on the sheet. We collected a couple of wheelbarrows full. The walnuts were still in their shucks, and if the shuck had cracked it was possible to remove the nut. Otherwise you throw away the nut; to prise out an unripe walnut is impossible. The shucked nuts were washed off in water and placed on sheets to dry out in the sunshine, being turned frequently. We had managed to collect these a few days before our return, so we had time to dry them in the good weather.

We visited Ingrid and Terry just before leaving, taking them some walnuts and explaining that these nuts were not ready to eat but would have to dry out further. We traded our news and updated them on the work in the cottage. They said they would visit next year and see how we were progressing.

The last job we undertook was to remove the two pairs of shutters at the front of the property. We had decided that as they were in urgent need of repairing and restoring, Ray could work on them in 'slow time' in England. In order to cover and protect the windows while we were absent, we had brought over two large sheets of plywood covered with matchboarding. These had already been stained and varnished and imitated shutters. For house insurance purposes, when leaving empty properties, windows have to be protected with shutters.

Marie-Odette and Sophie paid us a visit. After showing them our improvements in the new kitchen and the stained and varnished staircase, they expressed surprise at all our efforts. We gave them boxes of walnuts and said our goodbyes, promising we would see them again next year.

It was now Friday afternoon and our plan was to leave the next morning to drive to the ferryport. We packed up the trailer with all the usual tools and the returning shutters, covering and roping it securely. Inside the cottage we protected the mattresses with plastic coverings and put dust sheets over everything. We were up early to drain down the water system, making the property safe for the long winter months it had to remain empty.

Taking the usual route to St Malo, we arrived early evening and booked ourselves into a hotel. The day ferry on Sunday was an eight-hour crossing, but we had pre-booked ourselves a day cabin so we could have a sleep during the crossing. We were due back at work the following day. It had been so good to have extra time. The three-week stay had enabled us to meet our schedule, and we were very pleased with our efforts. Having the new kitchen in place, I was able to put the crockery and other items away into cupboards rather than wrapping everything in black plastic bags as on previous departures.

A plan was forming to slot in a visit before next May. Denny had informed us that his son was not going to do grass cutting as he now had a permanent job on a new airline route. We still had one more year before we were going to retire full-time. The idea was to bring over a ride-on lawn mower by trailer. We also wanted to hire a commercial machine that would sand up the floorboards throughout the loft and the end of the room in the dining area. Ray had used the belt sander on the kitchen floorboards, which had been very hard work.

Denny had advised us that before we continued to build rooms in the loft it would be advisable to spray the whole area with a special timber treatment. This would kill any woodworm and other wood-boring insects that might be a threat. We thought a weekend visit, staying overnight at the local hotel, might be the answer. We could do all three things in one fell swoop.

On our return I got a ferry booked for the following March. We were travelling over on a Thursday and would have Friday, Saturday and Sunday to complete the work.

Plumbing and planning

The project resumed on a chilly, bright morning in March 2002. The previous evening we had arrived at our cottage, uncoupled the trailer and left it on the driveway. Overnight we had enjoyed the comfort of the hotel above the café in Aubeterre. Log fires, a tasty meal and the friendliness of the staff made a good start to our busy few days. After breakfast we returned to the cottage, having collected fresh bread and cakes from the local *pâtisserie* to keep our energy levels up during the day.

Wearing our old clothes, the first job was to unload the new ride-on mower from the back of the trailer. It had been possible to drive the mower on the trailer with the aid of ramps, but to offload the vehicle was more complicated. It necessitated removing the trailer wheels to lower it enough to roll the mower off by hand. After a struggle we were successful and ready to start cutting the lawns, and the wheels were replaced on the trailer. The floor sanding machine, hired in England, was taken inside the cottage.

Although there was a keen wind, the sky was cloudless and the sun was shining. The grass surrounding the property was dry and it seemed a good opportunity to put the mower to use. If we managed to get a cut done in early March it might stop the grass getting out of hand before our visit in early May. Leaving Ray to continue with his mammoth task I started clearing furniture from the dining room so we could begin sanding.

After lunch we turned our attention to the floor-sander. Unsure of how many replacement belts would be required, we had hired plenty. Initially using the coarse grade, we soon removed the ingrained dirt. Then, using a medium belt, we began to smooth off the rough surface left by the coarse one. The machine had to follow along the line of the floor-boards, as deep scratching occurred if it went sideways across the floor. Where there was unevenness or any raised corner on a board the belt quickly snapped.

Realising that the flooring in the loft area was uneven and insecure, we had a problem. Before starting in this area Ray spent the afternoon hammering in raised nail heads, removing various staples and refixing any loose boards in preparation for our return the next day.

During the afternoon Denny visited us, keen to see the mower we had brought over from England. They sold ride-on mowers in France but they were much larger models with heavy cutting blades, and therefore quite expensive. He showed keen interest in the commercial sander; by investing in one himself he visualized undertaking similar work for his clients in France.

He explained that he would soon be beginning the necessary plumbing work to get the existing sewerage and waste from the present bathroom to the new septic tank. He would divert the external sewerage pipe by extension and cutting a hole through the outside kitchen wall (below floor level). The pipe would run under the floorboards straight through the kitchen and continue through the room we used as our bedroom to the far wall. Another hole would be cut through the external wall (below floor level) as the new tank was situated a metre from this wall. This enabled a straight run from entry to exit; there was plenty of depth between the earth and the floorboards to allow a sufficient drop in the pipe for the flow. It all sounded fairly feasible and we were assured that when we came back in May it would be completed.

We returned early on the Saturday to begin sanding the floor in the loft area. In some areas it was difficult to get close to the sides because the wiring feeding the downstairs lighting was tucked under capping running across the loft. We removed some capping to allow access, but some areas would have to be tackled later with the hand-held belt sander. Overall the whole area came up amazingly clean; our next problem was to keep it from getting dirty again. With the forthcoming work, plasterboard to be cut for the walls and ceilings, staining all exposed beams and finally painting and decorating, the newly-cleaned floor would definitely need protection. Luckily Denny had advised us to save the thick cardboard packaging from the kitchen units. This would provide a practical protective covering. Sure enough, there was enough strong cardboard to cover the whole of the loft area.

We had begun to take his advice before disposing of anything, and we found it amazing how many items could be recycled. For example, before they had done the work in the loft area they had removed the glass fibre which covered the floor. It was now rolled into six very large bundles and stored over the workshop roof. We would probably have thrown it out. He had told us it didn't appear to have been put down that long ago, and we should use it between the rafters before fixing the plasterboard to give insulation to the ceiling. From then on we have saved numerous items that have been given a second life.

On the Sunday, the last day of our mini-visit, we intended to follow more advice given by Denny. Protection was required on the exposed woodwork throughout the cottage. Although we had a certificate proving that no termites were present, there was evidence of live woodworm in the loft area, so we intended to undertake a spraying to protect against woodworm and other more serious wood-boring insects for a further ten years. Previously we had purchased some large cans of Xylophene from the bricolage. Judging by the range of wood treatment products on sale, it must be a common practice in France. Xylophene is highly toxic and on no account must the fumes be inhaled, so with this in mind, and because we would be working in a confined space for the whole day, we had purchased two (very expensive) protective chemical masks.

Our plan was to use our workshop round the back for the day, retreating for our coffee and lunch breaks out in the fresh air and eventually to change into fresh clothes before returning back to the hotel that night. By the end of the spraying the house would be so toxic it would not be safe to remain inside. Denny had been quite insistent about the dangers of undertaking spraying; he had known at least two cases of people who had ended up in hospital through inhalation of these fumes.

As on the previous two days, we purchased groceries and arrived early at the cottage. We needed to complete the whole job in one day. We changed into our protective boiler suits in the workshop and left our clothes, food and crockery, along with an electric kettle ready for later.

Ray opened one of the cans of liquid, then carefully poured it into two of the five-litre plastic cans which are normally used for spraying garden crops. The worst thing I remember about the job was having to wear the protective mask. These were adjusted individually to fit tightly over the face, not allowing in any air. Ray helped me to get my mask fitted and get relaxed with breathing. He then went into fits of laughter. "If only you could see yourself, you look hilarious!" he laughed.

I suppose I did, being covered in a pair of men's green overalls, a funny hat and protective shoes. Once the mask was on your face you could not speak and it was extremely heavy.

By now he had finished laughing and was beginning to realise how difficult it was having this monstrous thing covering your face. I had assisted him in pulling his straps tight, but with my mask already on we could not converse at all. We both looked as though we had come from the MoD to embark on a dangerous mission. Communication had to be by tapping the shoulder and making signs.

We proceeded to the loft area, starting at the far end and taking a side each. It was a time-consuming job as there were so many beams and rafters, and you had to keep stopping to pump up the can to get the pressure through the spray. The long nozzle reached in between the beams high up and hidden away from view. The new windows in the loft were wide open to let out the fumes.

It was a beautiful sunny March day with a gentle fresh wind blowing, and we could not have picked a better day for this sort of job. Breathing OK through the masks, which had large chemical filters each side, we felt completely protected. We continued without stopping to lunchtime, successfully covering all the ceiling beams and the upright supports, including the replacement ones for the iron rods. So far Ray had refilled the spray cans about five times from the large chemical containers.

When we retired to the workshop I could not wait to pull off my mask, which by now was really hurting. The masks had marked our faces with lines where they had fitted so tightly. We changed out of our overalls, as we could smell the chemical fumes on them. We allowed ourselves about an hour to have a rest and discuss how it was going so far.

We had used up two large containers of chemical. On opening the third container, which was by a different manufacturer, we noticed that the consistency of the product was different. Obviously all the instructions on the can were in French, but it would seem the product had to be painted on and not sprayed. This was about to bring the operation to an abrupt halt; it had been going fine up to now. We were done for! We had no paintbrushes as all our tools are returned home after each trip. The remainder of the job was to thoroughly soak all the loft floorboards and the newly-sanded floor area downstairs.

We used our initiative. As we had two long-handled brooms, the answer seemed to be to pour the chemical into a washing-up bowl and brush the liquid into the floorboards with brooms. Again we covered ourselves in overalls, protective glasses, gloves, and hats and reluctantly masked up. No way did I want to put that mask on my face but it was essential, as by now the fumes were very strong inside the house.

We soaked the floorboards with the liquid until the loft area was finally finished, then repeated the process on the floorboards downstairs until we were satisfied that no crawling or flying wood-boring insects would survive penetration of the chemical or, indeed, in the fumes from it.

We retreated to clean ourselves up in the workshop and I literally tore the mask from my face; it was really painful where it had been clamped on. Although they had been essential for the job, I hoped we would never have to use them again. Our overalls were then sealed up in plastic bags and packed in the trailer along with the sanding machine, ready for our return journey. We would renew the brooms and washing-up bowls on the next visit; they had served their purpose and enabled us to continue. All the contaminated items were locked away inside the 'cycle shed' with the old chemical containers; we would take all this rubbish to the déchetterie next spring.

It was now about six in the evening and we were looking forward to returning to the hotel for a soak in a nice hot bath. I quickly used the toilet before we left, holding my breath while inside the house; it was reeking of fumes and not the place to be. Locking the front door, I escaped back to the workshop. We were very satisfied with our few days and although feeling quite tired after all the hard work we coupled up the trailer and returned to Aubeterre.

On May 1st, with the trailer stacked full of the usual tools and materials, we set off again. On arrival we were amazed at the length of the grass. Could it possibly have grown that much since our first cut with the ride-on mower in early March? We would have to get cutting soon.

As we entered the house there appeared to be no smell at all from our spraying efforts. This was a relief, as we were going to be living and sleeping there for the next three weeks.

Denny had recently been working at the cottage, coupling up the new under-floor sewerage pipe from the toilet in the bathroom area through to the new septic tank. On testing the water flow he had discovered leaks. The winter had turned very cold after our visit in March and the compression joints had not stood up to the extremes. Various washers on the taps were leaking. The bathroom floor was very wet, with a large puddle under the wall-mounted water heater. The main problem was that a nut had sheared off inside the water heater and it was leaking through the gap. Until Ray fixed this we were without any hot water. Obviously this was a priority.

The heater was drained down and after undoing all the nuts the element could be removed, along with bucket after bucket of old limescale. No wonder the heater had weighed a ton when we tried to mount it on the wall. It was a miracle it ever worked. The broken nut was not metric but an old imperial measurement, and nothing similar could be found in the plumbing section at the bricolage. Fortunately Ray managed to replace it with one he found in a large jar of spare assorted nuts and washers he kept amongst his tools, otherwise we would have had to replace the heater there and then. Our plans for a new larger heater would materialize when the new plumbing went in for the future bathroom. At present we could not possibly know where it would be sited, only that it would be upstairs and not in the small existing bathroom area.

So our first four days were spent, yet again, in the old bathroom. Would that room ever be finished? Also, to cap it all, the new plumbing done by Denny from the toilet was leaking. He had not allowed enough gradient from the external sewerage pipe to take away the flow of water. So Ray had to drill out another large hole through the outside wall and make good all the jointing. The first week had almost passed, and we had not even started our planned schedule.

At the weekend Ray attempted to mow the front lawn. His first use of the mower had been back in March, using the blades on the high setting because of the unevenness of the ground. He checked for large stones and debris hidden in the grass. The unevenness of the area posed a problem, nearly throwing him off the mower several times. Finally, using his new strimming machine, he could remove long grass. He managed to reclaim a new area around the briar-bound shrubs.

We now had the beginnings of a garden. Being May the fruit trees were in full leaf, along with the early-flowering shrubs. The lilac trees along the front boundary were in blossom and looked a picture in white, soft lilac and deep mauve. We were lucky to have inherited such established trees. The pear tree and cherry tree on the front lawn would, after pruning, yield fruit in later years.

The temporary shutters Ray had fitted over the front windows had been removed shortly after our arrival, so before we left he had to refit the original shutters. After spending many hours over the winter months in England he had successfully stripped the old paintwork and repaired the damaged wood. Sections were replaced with seasoned oak he had obtained at a reclamation wood yard. They had been undercoated and painted a carefully chosen Buckingham green. We felt this colour would contrast well when the outside walls of the cottage were eventually painted a golden creamy colour.

We intended to bring over some tubs of stone paint which would refresh the existing dirty Tyrolean finish which made the cottage look so forlorn and gloomy. Also the flaking light blue paint on all the soffits and bargeboards did nothing to enhance the outside.

With the Velux windows in the loft giving plenty of light, we could see that the roof leaked in a few places when it rained heavily. The tiles were exposed on the underside, there being no roof felt. Odd glimpses of daylight were visible here and there. This troubled us, knowing we would be lining out the roof. We wanted felt under the tiles before embarking on fixing a new ceiling. We had seen a local *maçonnaire couverture* (roof installer) advertised locally and travelling to his address, we had found his house set amid woodland. After an encounter with a ferocious dog, an elderly woman appeared (probably his mother). I just about gathered from her French that he was away on holiday. Also she said we should have gone to his work site, and named the village. Eventually we found his yard, with evidence of piles of tiles and heavy tractors, and knew the maçonnaire would be available from next Monday.

Knowing we would shortly need some gravel for cement work outside, we decided to get this in our trailer. One scoop at the bricolage was a metric tonne. The scoop was skilfully delivered by the operator of the machine, accurately dumping it in the centre of the trailer. There was still some space left, so we signalled for another half load to be added. As we watched the trailer suddenly dropped, the tyres completely flat. The extra weight was just too much. Ray had forgotten to pump extra air to allow for the load. He began to unbolt the spare wheel attached to our trailer.

"What are we going to do?" I said, feeling very stupid standing by the useless trailer in the middle of the builders' yard. "Will we have to tip it all out?"

"You'd have a job to do that" said Ray. "No, we'll take the spare wheel to a garage, they have a special high pressure pump. We'll put the spare on the trailer, then take that wheel to the garage to do the same."

"That's going to take hours" I said. "It'll be lunchtime soon and the garage will shut. Oh God, it means we'll be here well into the afternoon".

What a stupid situation we had got ourselves into. Meanwhile the chap who had served us had sized up the situation. He shouted at us, "Mon dieu, oh la la! Vous avez un problème. Attendez, s'il vous plaît."

He left us and went off to assist another customer with his scoop machine. Ray carried on with getting the wheel uncoupled. Then the man returned to us, saying something about "le camion avec la pompe" (lorry with a pump).

"Un moment" he said. He started walking over to a large lorry at the back of the yard.

"Hang on, I think he's going to help us" I said to Ray. "He's fetching that lorry, and it sounded as if he said something about a pump."

The big lorry pulled alongside our trailer and he unravelled the air pump kept inside the lorry. Using the power from the lorry he blasted air into our two flat tyres. The trailer was roadworthy again. Thankfully we had been saved the arduous and time-consuming job of sorting ourselves out of the problem. We thanked him and after a lot of persuasion insisted he take a five-euro note for all his troubles.

That September we intended to plant 55 tiny cuttings of *Thorna placatia* trees around the edge of our lawn area, providing us with a mini-boundary to the acre and south side of the property. We planned to let them grow only to a low height. The ground in September would be far too hard to dig holes, remembering the struggle in planting our apple trees last September. So each morning we would rise early and dig out ten holes. The earth was saved and the hole filled with a plastic bag full of newspaper to keep it intact. Judging by the evidence of constant molehills around the property, the holes would have disappeared after a few months. We completed the task during our stay, but not without a huge effort as the ground proved very tough in places.

We also managed to cut back the overgrown privet hedge running along the north side. This was a mammoth task, as it was completely out of shape and trailing into the ditch. Fortunately, the ditches and verges had recently been cut with a special machine by a man from Le Mairie. After he had completely cleared out the ditch we could at least stand down it to cut back the privet.

The electricity meter at the side of the ditch was on a high pole. The meter, at a height of two metres, was completely covered in ivy and the reading obscured. The ivy stem causing this growth, was at the base of the pole and was much thicker than my wrist. After putting a saw through it close to the base we could only hope it would eventually die back and expose the meter. It was far too entwined to remove. We were surprised that EDF, our electricity supplier, had not complained; they must have been taking readings, as we were receiving the bills.

On the Monday we visited the roofing specialist, to be greeted by the owner and his brother. Partners in the business, they provided a roofing service around the area. Fortunately the brother spoke a little English, so we explained that we wanted felt put under our tiles. They agreed to visit us later in the week.

The leaks were finally sorted in the bathroom and the water heater appeared to have settled down, apart from the odd drip. It seemed safe to re-stick the floor tiles which had lifted due to being soaked from the leaks.

On this visit we had planned to finish the kitchen, moving the sink from the old kitchen up to the new area. After a careful measurement we discovered it was too large to cut into the new worktop positioned over the sink units. We could still use the mixer tap, but it would mean a visit to Ribérac to choose a suitable sink.

Another day was wasted searching for sinks; we could not find the right size in Ribérac, so we had to go into Périgueux. The large Mr Bricolage was no longer located on the outskirts, in the industrial area. Notices displayed outside gave directions to the new premises. Eventually we found a newly-emerging industrial site in Busillac, a village to the east of Périgueux. It did prove a useful excursion as we came across an electrical wholesaler where we could get all the equipment required for the planned rewire.

Returning with a new sink, more adaptable to the corner area, our plan was to cut this into the worktop the following day. This would allow us to continue using the existing sink until the new one was ready. But nothing to do with water ever went smoothly for us. The next problem was that the new sink had a square overflow but the necessary waste fixing was not included in the pack. Hence another trip, another morning wasted, before the sink could be commissioned.

Initially we had used a short length of cooker cable from the meter to our cooker, but now we had to resite the cooker in the new kitchen. The new cooker cable had to be taken from the meter through the cavity wall up into the loft. It then needed to run the entire length of the loft down to the other end of the cottage. This was half a day's work. We then moved the cooker to the allotted space between the units. I now proceeded to move all the provisions, along with cooking utensils, into the new area. I could now cook and work in this area, but until the sink was finally plumbed I was still washing up and fetching water for cooking from the other end of the kitchen. Still, it was progress. I was so happy to have a proper kitchen area at last; it was marvellous to have all the crockery, cutlery and pans permanently in the new cupboards.

The two roofers turned up and explained that it would not be possible just to put felt under the existing tiles. It would mean a new roof. This dismayed us, as we had not planned to renew the roof. We asked them to prepare a quotation and said we would collect it from their yard in a few days' time. We could only assume that it would prove far too costly and considered other possibilities to repair the leaks.

The next couple of days saw the sink finally sorted. We now had the new kitchen up and running. This freed up the other end of the room to become the new dining room. Now the old kitchen units could be removed. The large mosaic worktop was smashed into pieces for easy removal. The cupboards were dismantled and stored in the cycle shed. Again another recycling plan, as they would (when spare time permitted) be reassembled in the workshop for storing Ray's tools.

The bare walls behind the units were in a disgusting state, especially the corner behind the old sink area. There had been no backs on the cupboard bases so after removal we found many old mice nests, along with plenty of skeletons. I felt grateful I had not stored anything inside, suspecting all along that mice had inhabited them at some time. I scrubbed the walls down twice before I was happy to emulsion over to erase the dirty marks.

Now a very strange incident happened concerning a pigeon. Opposite, in the neighbour's garden, was an old dovecote built on high supports and disguised by a wisteria shrub. It seemed evident that it was now inhabited by pigeons, which often woke us with their cooing. So it was quite a common sight to see pigeons flying around our cottage.

As we were working in the old kitchen area, engrossed in cleaning, there was a sudden bang against the window. As I turned to the window I could see a pigeon flying off. I thought at first he had misjudged his flight path and hit the glass by mistake, but then I saw him return. Flying up to the window again, he flapped his wings. He repeated this several times. Then, seeing me through the glass, he landed on the large white ledge and pecked at the window.

By this time I had called Ray to watch the antics of this comical bird. Ray had kept pigeons in his youth and knew a lot about their habits, but he had not seen this behaviour before.

"Do you think he is trying to tell us something?" I asked, to which Ray replied "Like what?"

"Why would he keep doing that?" I said. With that the pigeon again fluttered against the window.

"I am sure he is trying to get our attention" I said. With that I went up to the loft area. It was empty, with daylight from the new Velux windows which were tightly closed. I then saw a sparrow flying around. Seeing me, he came to a stop perching on one of the beams. He was very frightened and trembling. I opened the small new window which led out over the workshop, then returned downstairs. Looking upstairs five minutes later, the bird had gone. How it had entered the loft area was a mystery, probably through a small gap impossible for him to go back through.

Returning downstairs, there was no sight of the pigeon at the window. Had the pigeon heard that little bird's cries for help, then tried to attract our attention? I like to think that was the case. We have never had a pigeon flap at the window again from that day to this.

With the corner cleared, we found that hidden under the kitchen cupboards was a quarry-tiled floor. It would lend itself to a character base to site the new log-burning stove. We visualised a brick surround with a heavy oak mantelshelf. Above this we would clad the wall with old seasoned oak for a backdrop, creating a focal point in the room.

We had already decided that the ceiling with the old polystyrene tiles had to go; Ray then set about removing these. It was good fun pulling down the tiles and plasterboard along with the inevitable mice nests. Amazing the places they get into, no wonder the neighbour insisted on putting down plenty of powders! I vowed we would eventually fill up every possible gap or entry point so we would not have to live so close to mice again. The first plan had already been put into place. The airbrick holes around the walls outside the house were quite large and would have allowed all sorts of creatures to enter under the space between the earth and floorboards. These four ventilation holes had been covered with fine mesh and then ornamental black wrought iron gratings. Now we were safe in the knowledge that no mice, snakes or rats could possibly get under the house.

With the old ceiling gone we could see the underside of the loft floorboards. These were set between the twelve supporting beams which ran across the room. At the moment these beams were very rough and hairy. They needed sanding smooth using the belt-sander, then distressing at the edges to make them look old. After staining with dark stain it would create the illusion of oak; several coats of varnish would seal them, giving a satin finish. Although we had no stone walls, we would be having exposed beams throughout the cottage.

The rubbish from the ceiling filled bags and bags of plastic sacks ready to take up to the déchetterie on our next visit, along with the old smashed-up worktop. Fortunately we had covered the newly-sanded floor area with dust sheets. This area was washed down and covered with cardboard and dust sheets for permanent protection. The room was now empty, apart from the small table we still had our meals on. The new table and pine dresser would remain stored away until we finished the room. There was so much work planned for this room. Because of the height of the ceiling, now even higher with the old tiles removed, we planned to run a shelf around the room a couple of feet down from the beams. This would balance out the room and it could be used for ornaments to give the room some character.

Our intention was to plasterboard in between the exposed beams. This would cover the underside of the loft floorboards and be finished with textured paint to match the ceiling over the new kitchen area. We still had to remove the right-hand side of the new staircase to win back more floor area in the loft space. The supporting beams that had been cut away to allow entry in the ceiling would have to be reinstated. This work was planned for the following year, after I had finally retired at the end of December.

We had plans to kick-start the work after my retirement by arriving in February and staying until late May, allowing four months to really get involved. So far our efforts on the holiday breaks had only accomplished minimum effort on several projects.

On the Tuesday of our last week, I went into the small town of Saint Aulaye to collect some provisions at the little mini market, which stocked everything you could wish for, except fresh milk, hence the weekly trip to Ribérac. The majority of French people seem happy to use UHT milk or long-life bio-milk.

On returning, I decided to call in at the roofers' yard to see if the estimate was ready. I collected the envelope from the office and returned to the car. I thought I would just have a quick look and was amazed. The total cost was half of what we were expecting, yet the quotation was very comprehensive. All the work involved was explicitly detailed, including removal of the obsolete chimney we had blocked off, repairing the woodwork under the soffits and the gaping hole opposite the laurel tree. The usual French terms applied - a thirty percent deposit and the rest on completion.

Ray, too, was pleasantly surprised at the cost. Being close to midday I telephoned them to say we could come and see them when they re-opened after lunch. On returning we were greeted by the owner, who spoke only French, but it was clear we were happy with the price and we were given a date in August when the work could be carried out. We paid our deposit and gave him our spare key. Another reason we felt happy to entrust them with the work was they had just completed re-roofing a house in our village. As far as we could see their workmanship looked very good.

Ray had thought of using our September visit to do the rewiring. Before we could really go any further with work at the cottage we had to install a new lighting system and sockets. Ray had rigged up some temporary ones in the kitchen area, but I had to keep juggling between sockets to use the appliances. The problem was that the French wiring system was completely different from that in England. Ray's plan was to check up on this during the summer months by way of books and the internet. It soon became clear that our three-week stay would not be enough time to complete a rewire. It was definitely a job for after we retired. Therefore, we promised ourselves more time off in September and a chance to enjoy a rest.

On arrival in September we were greeted with a beautiful new roof. The workmanship looked great; a solid fixing of cement for the ridge tiles, as well as the hip returns either end of the cottage. The only problem was an enormous crater about three metres square on the edge of the front lawn. Evidently this had been made by a tractor sinking into a wet lawn. The moulds of the large tyres were baked hard and deep. Close to the house there were other deep holes in the grass where the tiles had been placed in high piles for the men to work.

But the main thing was that the roof was excellent. Upstairs in the loft area it was all nicely lined out with felt. Obviously, only to be expected, there was a large amount of clearing up to do on the loft floor along with the tile chips and debris around the outside. We just had to repair the crater in the lawn.

We had always promised that one day we would get a wellhead to place over our *puits* along the side of the property. Originally every house in the village would have had its water pumped up from underground via the well, but now the wells were mostly used in emergencies when the supply was cut off, which often happens.

We grabbed our chance when we came across a special offer - a lovely creamy coloured wellhead with a wrought-iron top. On collection it was cleverly packed and covered on a pallet, which was loaded onto our trailer by fork-lift truck. On returning to our driveway we uncoupled the trailer and proceeded to dismantle the package. I was standing in the trailer helping to unpack it when suddenly my weight tipped the balance of the trailer, which upended, throwing me and the centre of the well off the trailer. I fell on top of it, fortunately landing on grass.

"Lucky it's not broken" said Ray. "Are you OK?"

After helping me up, Ray managed to roll the wellhead onto a trolley with wheels; he then positioned it round the side. I escaped with only bruising on this occasion. For my sympathy and thanks I was duly reprimanded for standing in the wrong place and tipping the trailer. This happened on many, many occasions and I would come off the worse while assisting.

Judy told me that she too was often called upon to lift amazingly heavy objects and stand for hours with hands in the air supporting brackets and beams while they were fixed into place, and all for the love of a French cottage. Their latest venture had been a request for Denny to get two pillars for their driveway on which to hang a large wooden gate, giving extra security to their property. On arriving from England they found Denny had left them two 40-centimetre-square, five-foot-high solid wooden supports which looked as though they should have been used for the entrance to a château. Brian and Judy together could not even lift them, let alone position them for cementing. When we visited them they described how they had manoeuvred these objects by rolling them over and over and used rope to winch them into an upright position. Judy put her back out during this escapade and received very little sympathy, but like a true trouper she was gearing up for their next project.

Shortly after arriving we were invited to afternoon tea again with Ingrid and Terry. It was lovely to relax in their beautifully-kept garden. They talked about friends nearby with whom they share different hobbies and pastimes. Perhaps in the future we too could become accepted into the local life. Ingrid suggested we get some soil ordered to fill in our crater on the lawn. She promised to arrange it with a young lady who lived in one of the cottages in our hamlet; she happened to work for a local road building firm supplying gravel, sand and stones.

We had bought over our 55 tiny conifer saplings, which were watered daily. Now we had to find the holes we had prepared in the spring. It was only the fact that we had filled each hole with newspaper in a plastic bin liner that enabled us to find them. The landscape of the garden was so easily rearranged with long grass, weeds and the constant molehill upheaval. Over the summer period the whole area dried out in the heat with large cracks in the earth. The bags duly removed, we could fill the holes with water and start planting. We collected the soft earth from the molehills around the cottage and mixed it with compost and fertilizer. Each hole was filled around a tiny tree supported by a large bamboo stick. They looked lost in among the grassy landscape, but hopefully the rains of winter would keep them watered and help them to become established in the coming months.

We had often experienced the sudden storms that blow up in the Dordogne. The heat of the summer gradually builds; the air is still and oppressive. The sky darkens and the rumbling of an approaching storm is heard in the distance. Suddenly the heavens open and there is no time to run for cover before you are soaked. But then, as quickly as it blew up, it is over and the sunshine is out again drying up the puddles.

A full-blown *tempête*, as it is called by the locals, is something else. Indeed it is quite an experience. Our first encounter with one of these dramatic storms occurred one evening after a long dry spell of weather. Contrary to the usual stillness before a storm there was a strong lift in the air and a massive gust of wind. Hot, warm air was swirling around, gradually gathering force until everything in its path was scattered, bending the branches, flattening grass and twisting clothes over the washing line. Now was the time to batten down. Shutters were drawn over windows as *l'orage* (storm) gathered force. First came the very large spots of rain, which quickly dried on the warm ground. Then as the storm rolled in the rain lashed horizontally in the wind. In the distance the sky lit up with a massive flash of lightning, followed a few seconds later by the crash of thunder. These flashes intensified, drawing closer and coming from all angles, forking from the sky and bolting into the earth, with terrific rolls of thunder following.

We watched keenly, fascinated as the dark sky was made as bright as daylight and experiencing the most ear-splitting thunderclaps right overhead. It rumbled around and the rain intensified, drumming with deafening ferocity on the roof. Then it slowly subsided into normal rain. It rumbled on, the lightning passing as the storm moved across the countryside. Then without warning another flash and with no time to count the seconds there was an ear-shattering clap of thunder, like some mythological Greek god dropping a fifty-ton stone on a slab of marble, right over the house. My heart missed a beat.

These storms eventually subside, but although dying away, they may keep rumbling on for another couple of hours. The next morning you survey the damage. Torn-up trees and broken branches lie scattered around the land, such is the power of *la tempête*.

Our next visit would be the start of our full-time retirement and the chance to really start making an impression. I calculated that since purchasing our cottage in 2000 the amount of time we had actually spent there was only sixteen weeks in total. Our efforts had created improvements - a new bathroom and kitchen, decoration of the temporary lounge and a general clean up. Although we had resorted to professional help for the new roof, staircase, four windows, septic tank and driveway this provided a framework for us to work on. All future restoration would be undertaken solely by us.

On my return to work after our holiday at the cottage my colleagues would say, "Have you nearly finished now?" With so many programmes on television showing people transforming places in a matter of weeks, workmates could not understand why we were taking so long. My explanation was that it was a project to keep us active and occupied in the early years of retirement. Ray estimated it would take five years from 2003 to complete the structural work.

The intention to arrive mid-February meant the weather could be fairly chilly. Ray intended to get two of the storage heaters installed before this visit ended to ensure we had warmth to work in. He began by fixing a temporary feed into the meter. On taking over the electricity account we inherited a cheap off-peak tariff used between 11 pm and 6.30 am, which would enable us to charge night storage heaters, the appliances giving off the stored heat throughout the following day. We had already purchased four second-hand heaters in England which had been dismantled. So far, each pull of the trailer had contained several of the internal blocks and two outer cases.

The two replaced shutters at the front of the property were a vast improvement after all the repair work lavished on them. Ray now removed the two remaining sets of shutters from the windows at each side of the cottage ready to take back with us. He could work on them during the winter months. Before we left he would replace the shutters with the temporary ones, as on the last visit.

We tidied up the garden and knuckled the two front trees. All the branches were cut back to the trunks and taken with other garden cuttings for a large bonfire burn-up. We managed to collect some walnuts and dry them out in the sunshine to take back to England.

The only problem was that the soil had not yet turned up. I reminded Ingrid and Terry that we were leaving in two days, and she promised to chase up the firm.

On our last morning, the trailer had been loaded and we were getting the house closed down for winter. We would be ready to leave in two hours. Then at 8 am our five tonnes of soil arrived. It was offloaded into the crater, but obviously had to be spread around. We quickly changed into old clothes and started to work on the pile. Half an hour later it started to drizzle, after three weeks of perfect weather. The soil was gradually starting to cling together and the clods made it difficult to spread. But we could not leave it, as on our return it would be a solid heap full of weeds. We pressed on.

After two hours we had managed to level off the area, blending it into the lawn. Then we began wheelbarrowing various amounts of soil to fill the other holes by the house. The rain got heavier and we were soon completely soaked. Finally I shook two boxes of grass seed over the fresh earth, saying a small prayer that it would grow during the following months.

There was just time to take a shower and change before locking up the house and heading off to the ferryport.

La vie française

The ferry back to France was booked for 18th February 2003. During the winter months we had been accumulating items for the trip. The trailer was full, its cargo including the remaining bricks for the fireplace and heater blocks, along with the last two storage-heater cases. On board was a small deep freeze, essential for storing bulk purchases of meat. This would make shopping more economical when living in France for several months at a time. We were loaded with essential wood for architraves, skirting-boards, door stops and surrounds for the new Velux windows. Although we would purchase the majority of materials in France, Ray knew that by taking specific amounts of lighter wood from his supplier in England, we would save money and time searching for it in France.

I had finished with my firm just before Christmas. Enjoying all the customary farewells and promises of keeping in touch, I now could begin to enjoy retirement full time. But really I was gearing up to a very busy year ahead indeed. No more sitting at a desk - our project would mean quite a physical change for me.

In January we had purchased a new car. The Peugeot 406 saloon which had been the mainstay of our trips was traded in on a good deal for a new 406 estate. This car was very spacious; with the back seats folded down we could take at least four large suitcases of essential clothes and bed linen which would remain in the cottage. Smaller boxes of tools were included in the car, which freed up space in the trailer. After this visit Ray would have assembled the old kitchen units in his workshop and could permanently leave tools in these cupboards, having gradually duplicated them so his newer ones remained in England.

A lot of thought went into closing down our English house for four months. Apart from draining down the water and switching off everything electrical, we made the house as secure as possible. Utility bills were converted to direct debit so we would not come back to unpaid demands.

On a bright and unseasonably warm February day we set off to the ferryport. The crossing was calm for the time of year and we arrived early the following evening. It did not feel as cold in the cottage as we had anticipated. It was still daylight and we were able to uncouple the heavy trailer and unload the tools and equipment from the car, reinstating the back seats. Spare storage heater blocks and the bricks for the fireplace were stacked into corners of the cycle shed. The new deep freeze was brought inside and sited in the kitchen area under the stairs.

As usual we removed the plastic protection from the mattress and pillows, making the bed with an electric blanket and thick duvet. Ray switched on the two night-storage heaters assembled on our previous visit; we hoped by morning they would have started to warm up the cottage.

In our usual café in Aubeterre we enjoyed the warmth from the log-burning stove. We were not alone, surrounded by many other people dining on a winter's night in the middle of February. As we left the sky was clear with a bright moon shining; there was a lovely sweet scent of oak wood burning in the evening air, a magical smell which always provokes images of France.

Now both fully retired, we could carry out the plan to commence restoration on a much higher level. This visit was for fifteen weeks and we hoped to get the ground floor into a decent habitable state. Ray's first task was to turn the small triangular corner cupboard (in our temporary lounge) into an airing space. By installing shelves and a small tubular heater it would provide essential space for the storage of bedding and towels.

At Ribérac we stocked up on provisions and ordered a washing machine, essential for our long stay. Previous short holiday trips had not included washing dirty clothes; all soiled bed linen had returned home with us. I chose the French style, which was a top-loader, slimmer than a front door model. This would conveniently sit alongside the end of the kitchen units. It made for easy plumbing connections under the sink.

Eventually, after building the proposed new bathroom,

the plan was to convert the downstairs bathroom to a utility room, installing the washing machine and deep freeze. But not for quite a while!

The washing machine arrived the following week. The delivery man shook hands in the customary way, insisting on wheeling the machine to its new home. He then unpacked it, not leaving until we had confirmed we were happy. This seems the common practice on appliances delivered to your home in France.

Enjoying dry sunny days, we set about clearing the ground around the walnut trees. Because of shortage of time on our holiday visits, we had rarely ventured down to the boundary where the walnut trees grew. Several clumps of brambles over two metres high and covering most of the ground around the walnut trees were hacked out and burned on three large bonfires. This complete execution of the briars took much longer than anticipated. It is time consuming handling these monsters. They spring back to slap you in the face and claw at your clothes, so it has to be done with caution.

Finally we tried to mow around the area. It was too uneven for Ray to use the ride-on, so we decided to invest in a small petrol mower which I could operate to do these uneven areas around the trees. After two full days of hard physical labour our efforts were rewarded. The area was transformed. We could actually see what trees we possessed and the walnut harvest would be made much easier.

We decided the first major project would be the reinstatement of the supporting beam across the dining room. This had been cut out by Denny to install the right-hand side of the staircase. Using adjustable Acrow props to support the end of the existing beam, Ray removed the last tread of the staircase. He managed to reinstate the original beam, which luckily had been left in the loft. Sitting astride the adjacent beam using long coach bolts, he refixed the beam. He then reinstated the hole in the ceiling with new floorboarding in the loft. This floor area would provide the extra space needed to create a walk-in wardrobe in the new bedroom area.

We had often commented that we had never seen any local signs advertising eggs for sale. With so many chickens about we would have thought there would have been lots of opportunity to get new-laid eggs. One day an English couple renting a cottage in our hamlet, which had been their custom for many summers, told me they got eggs from the farmer's wife, Madame Sautet. "She will let you have some for a couple of euros" they said.

Sure enough Madame Sautet was happy to sell us a dozen eggs. The next morning we had boiled eggs for breakfast and the yolks were dark golden with an unbelievable delicious flavour. We hadn't tasted eggs like that for a long time. The following day I made a sponge cake. The yolks' colour made the cake dark yellow and with the special French *gateaux* flour the taste was far superior to my cakes in England. Needless to say, when in France from that day to this, every fortnight I am at her kitchen door, egg box in hand to buy eggs.

Later I heard through another source that Madame Sautet's eggs are known to be superior. Is it because they are true 'scratch hens'? Perhaps she has a royal breed of hens; or is it some secret ingredient she puts in their food? Another French mystery.

Our itinerary for the next few months was to do the rewire and then concentrate on completely finishing the dining-room area. The idea was to work from 8 am to 5 pm each weekday. The weekend would be free for normal routine jobs, ie I would do the washing and cleaning Saturdays, while Ray would do lawns and other jobs outside the current project. Sundays were 'free time'. Theoretically a good idea, in practice not always possible!

Two internal doors taken home for refurbishment were returned this trip. They had been stripped of their old paint down to the natural pine. I set about staining them medium oak with a final coat of varnish. One was reinstated to the temporary lounge and the spare was kept for future use in the new rooms upstairs.

Just as we were thinking things were going smoothly, the water heater packed up. All the time and effort spent on moving and repairing this heater had been wasted. We had intended to purchase a new, larger heater, but not at this moment in time. So another day was lost visiting the commercial shopping centre on the outskirts of Périgueux to seek out the best buy. The most practical solution was a 200 litre tank, designed to be balanced on a special support. The overflow and various connections were positioned underneath. Luckily the massive tank just fitted in the back of the estate car, so we did not have to have it delivered.

The next problem was that it had to be sited up in the loft area, where the layout of rooms was unknown. It was an important decision, as the copper piping to the tank had to continue from the tank to the new bathroom area. This dilemma was resolved by measuring the tank and stand, when we discovered that it would only fit in one area which was just left of the staircase. The area behind the tank was exposed brickwork, the end wall of the cottage. This area was due to be battened, insulated and finished with plasterboarding when work started in the loft. Once the heater was in position it could not be moved, so we now had to insulate and plaster-board behind the new tank. Another two days' work.

The water heater was slowly manoeuvred up the stairs, Ray trying to drag it on a rope and me pushing from below. The next problem was to mount the tank onto the circular stand; no way could we lift it between us. Ray and another strong man would have easily done the job. Although I managed to assist with a lot of heavy lifting I was often limited on certain things. The problem was usually solved by Ray working out some ingenious way round the situation. This duly happened for the water heater and, at last, the tank was up on the stand.

I spent the next three days as a plumber's mate. The old heater had to be drained and disconnected and new copper piping connected to feed the existing downstairs bathroom from the new tank upstairs. Ray managed to get the new pipes into the wall cavity between dining room and bathroom and then site them around the walls, which would be covered with plasterboard, making a very neat job.

With all the problems we had incurred with plumbing so far at the cottage, I was very nervous about turning the water on. Two metres of pipe leading away from the tank were capped off. Small stop taps were included to avoid draining down the tank when future work was undertaken for the upstairs plumbing. The tank was slowly filled and each connection tested for leaks. After two days managing without water the job was successfully completed.

We were already two weeks into March when we commenced the rewire. Ray had done his homework via the internet and was happy in the knowledge that he could comply with the French wiring system. We made out a list of materials in French and visited the wholesale electrical supplier we had discovered near Périgueux on a previous trip.

Our French was still very poor, so we produced our typed list. I can still picture the assistant now, cigarette drooping from his mouth and not saying a word to us, briefly consulting the list, then fetching items. He would scratch his head, then disappear for some more items. Most were found, but they did not do three-pole switches and a few other items contrary to the French system. He gestured to us to suggest various alternatives. I felt embarrassed, as we could not explain in detail what we wanted. He was used to dealing with French electricians, not an English couple unable to converse in French.

Luckily, in England Ray had bought the two large consumer units needed for the job. He had ordered Hager, a make common in France which fully complied with regulations. Intending to install storage heaters, and never having seen any for sale in France, we knew it was going to be tricky ordering a special consumer unit for these. I was thankful we did not have to explain this item. Finally, we departed the car loaded with reels of cable and boxes of switches and sockets.

The rewire progressed slowly. I was in charge of pulling out all the existing cables, which were fed to the downstairs rooms from the loft area. The French system is not like a ring-main in England. All appliances have to be separately wired directly from the meter position. Ray had purchased the capping in England, and as each room was tackled the capping was positioned accordingly. The mains cable was much thicker than the English equivalent and it was difficult to get two wires into the capping, although we had brought a good choice of sizes. The French sockets are fairly flimsy compared to English ones and Ray found it very time-consuming wiring in the thick mains cable.

Two weeks into the work we were making good progress. It was a glorious morning in late March, the sun was shining and the windows were wide open. I saw our neighbour coming over to see us and went outside to talk to her. We were both looking through the window into the dining room area where Ray was working when he told us he had just seen a snake among the trailing cables strewn across the floorboards. Our neighbour said *le serpent* and *la couleuvre*, which, we now know, means grass snake. Ray then said he must have imagined it and carried on working.

The neighbour departed and I went inside to get some

lunch. Ray was convinced by now that he must have imagined it, but I was not so sure. I was in the kitchen area and as I looked between the end of the units and the fridge I saw the head of a snake, the rest of his body hidden behind the unit. I called Ray; he saw the head just before it disappeared.

The snake was hidden by the plinth in front of the units. Ray decided to remove the plinth at the far end by the sink, with the thought of chasing it out. On removing the plinth the snake had already fled up to that end; I shone a torch and could see to my amazement the full length of his body, well over a metre and a half in length.

We panicked. I ran over to my neighbour and kept saying "le serpent est dans la cuisine!" She responded by taking on my concern and replied "J'irai pour mon voisin" (I'll go for my neighbour). I returned to the kitchen, where Ray stood guard over the snake (it probably being far too frightened to move).

Eventually two men came from the village. One was the farmer, Monsieur Sautet, with his shotgun and the other an elderly gentleman who cycled up on his bicycle; we now know him as Monsieur Astier. On arriving he did not hesitate; he put his hand straight under the small open area and made a grab for the snake behind its head. Unfortunately, he did not grip it high enough and as he brought the snake out it turned its head and sunk his fangs into his hand. At the same time it curled its body around Monsieur Astier's arm. I had never seen an animal move so fast. Its body was wrapped around his wrist before you could blink. He didn't flinch, but held on tight to the snake and took it out of the house to the road. The farmer grabbed the tail and then proceeded to smash its head onto the tarmac, which killed it.

I then insisted Monsieur Astier let me put some ointment and a plaster over the fang marks on his hand. He kept making gestures about not making any fuss. After we had thanked him the best way we could in our limited French, he departed on his bicycle. I have since learned that grass snake bites are harmless; France has several other species of snake, but only the vipers are seriously poisonous.

It really gave us a scare at the time, not knowing what snake it was, and we were surprised by the length of its body. Later we realised it had come up the steps and through the front door. Ray had first seen it curled up alongside the cables strewn across the floor, and we assumed it thought the cables were other snakes. At that time of year the snake would have been searching for a mate. As it turned out, because it was a very warm spring that year, we were to encounter a few more grass snakes.

Needless to say we kept the front door closed after the incident; we left the key in the lock to enable easy access as it was the only entrance. The next few days I always looked under the bed and felt very jumpy thinking of snakes, but once we got immersed into the re-wire along with all its problems we soon forgot about the snake incident.

The job was completed after four weeks using up most of the materials and metres of capping. It was great to have sockets in the kitchen and not make do with makeshift cable extensions. It had necessitated a lot of planning as each socket had an individual cable which had to be returned to the meter box. Also provision had been made for the new sockets and lighting required up in the loft area. Necessary spare circuit breakers were allocated in the junction box; the mains leads and lighting cable were fed through to the upstairs. The downstairs was now finished, including three storage heaters permanently installed.

We then took a couple of days away for a short holiday to Monpazier, a beautiful medieval town built around a massive open square surrounded by ancient cloisters providing secret shopping arcades. This was to celebrate our wedding anniversary in early April. It was great to experience a new area in France and a chance to spend a day visiting the famous medieval town of Sarlat.

At one time the city would have been secure within the city's boundary walls. Now you find your way from modern roads and the surrounding village into a maze of streets leading to the very heart of the ancient town. Narrow passageways run between tall thirteenth-century houses built in warm coloured sandstone blocks, so tight together you could easily shake hands with the neighbour opposite through the tiny windows. Now it's a large tourist attraction with restaurants tucked in amongst the ancient buildings, their small outside tables spilling over onto the pavement area where you sit and watch modern life go by.

There were plenty of tiny souvenir shops selling a huge range of products, including *foie gras, confit de canard* and assorted pâté. Bottles of the local "vin" were exhibited in triple packs, or "supériorité crus" in wooden boxes. The choice of apéritifs applicable to the region was amazing. A local artist had an impressive studio and his paintings of the old city captured the atmosphere exactly. We invested in a limited edition print, a lovely reminder of our visit to this enchanting town.

By mid-April the weather was getting quite hot, with plenty of sunshine. I would have loved to spend more time outside cutting back the jungle of shrubs and foliage along the side of the property, but I had to resist, knowing we must press on with the enormous task of working on the beams and creating a new plasterboard ceiling.

As planned, the beams were going to be exposed. Ray used his belt-sander to make them smooth, taking off edges in places to give them a distressed look. Then we rigged up the large four-metre scaffold plank across the room, resting it on ladders either side. This enabled me to reach the beams to stain them with the dark oak before sealing them with the satin finish varnish. There were twelve beams to do and we lost count of the times the plank was moved backward and forwards under each beam to complete two coats of stain and three coats of varnish. While I had been undertaking this Ray had to box in the areas around the fireplace and where he had joined back the original beam and reinstated the hand rail across the empty right-hand side of the staircase to make it safe.

The word for a rubbish bin is *la poubelle*, but waste material is called *déchets*, hence the word *déchetterie*. The *déchetterie* is where the title of 'jobsworth' comes into its own in a big way. When we arrive with a trailer full of rubbish the uniformed men pounce earnestly, inspecting the contents. You lift the empty paint can and are about to throw it into the scrap metal bin. The man draws breath, shouts "non, non, non!" and points to the furthest corner of the yard, near the oil drums. He has assumed there may be remnants of paint, so you are watched while you march up to deposit your tin with the old paint pots. Having doubted your competence to match up your rubbish with his bins, he hovers, watching your every move.

More hesitation - you have light bulbs in with the empty wine bottles. "Non, non, non!" he says, pointing to the bulbs. He says a word in French. "Pardon?" I say. He repeats the word, pointing towards the area at the end of the tip. I am none the wiser, so I just wander off to the furthest corner again and gently place them on top of some boxes, hoping that when the men do their tour of inspection they will accommodate my defunct light bulbs.

Lastly, the old cable from the rewire is pulled out. We hesitate. Are we really going to strip the outer cover for the 'plastic' bin and the internal wire for the 'metal' bin? He gesticulates to the 'general rubbish'. Thank goodness for that.

Now that we are fully initiated, before any visit the rubbish is sorted for fast disposal. We are even recognised and acknowledged as regulars. No longer does the man hover over our trailer, unless of course his beady eye spots something he can recycle for himself.

The next major job was to install plasterboard between

the beams to form a new ceiling. The previous September we had taken delivery of a dozen sheets of plasterboard which we stored in the workshop along the back wall. The eight-foot sheets were propped up on their sides. They had been covered in plastic sheeting throughout the winter - on no account must the board get damp or it will crumble.

One by one we carried the eight-by-four sheets round to the front entrance, negotiating the small flight of steps. Then we proceeded to cut each one to size to fit between the beams. It was a time-consuming job as the space differed on each section. Also we had to move our scaffold plank up and down accordingly. Finally we had filled in each section.

Next we used textured paint to create a stipple finish to match the new ceiling we had created up the other end of the room. First the newly-stained beams had to be protected from being splashed with the textured paint and the white emulsion. Using masking tape, newspaper was placed over each side of the beams. Again manoeuvring the plank, we worked our way up and down the rows, painting the ceiling. Eventually, after completing the job, we removed the newspaper and stood back to see the finished look. Yes, we certainly had achieved the look we wanted. Our room now had exposed beams.

Finally we wanted to create a fifteen-centimetre wide shelf around the whole of the dining room. We had purchased second-hand oak from the reclamation yard at Wells, Somerset. With the electric plane Ray smoothed the wood, making a clean finish. He had already prepared and stained fancy-shaped supports for the shelf. We fixed the new shelf on the supports after staining and varnishing it the same colour as the beams. As the ceiling was now over ten feet in height the room could easily take a shelf sited a couple of feet down from the ceiling. This shelf would then display ornaments, which would give the room cottage character'.

It was now May and we had been in France almost twelve weeks. The weather had been warming up with plenty of sunshine which, in turn, had made the grass grow. We had already cut it a couple of times and it was gradually improving, but it was still very uneven and several times Ray had unbalanced himself on the ride-on mower. The molehills were back, appearing daily. So we collected up the large mounds of soil deposited by these hidden creatures happily living buried in our garden, and spread this in the dips, hoping to even out the lawn area.

The splendid weather continued and at weekends - my free time - I undertook garden duties, encouraging new grass by spreading seed on the earth from the molehills. I tackled the existing shrubs, hacking them back to a reasonable level and pulling out, where possible, the briars that grew up in the middle which choked life out of the bushes.

The roses that climbed up the side of the house were now coming into bloom, but they desperately needed to be cut back and tied for support. Even after spending a whole day hacking at the ivy spread across from the privet hedge, which completely covered the walkway round to the back of the cottage, it still looked overgrown and out of control. Meanwhile the large laurel tree continued to blot out light to the kitchen window and stunt growth to the surrounding shrubs. Perhaps some time in the future we would have a chance to remove it. Spare time was not available at present.

We now sat outside regularly for lunchtime snacks. Eagerly we took every opportunity to enjoy the sunshine and fresh air. The next major project was to install the fireplace. We knew we had only three more weeks at the cottage and we had to finish the dining room and kitchen areas by wallpapering and painting. The extra time spent installing the new water heater had set the original schedule back a week.

The installation of the fireplace would have to wait for our return in September. It was important that we finish the large room, as our son and his partner Sally would be staying at the cottage in July for two weeks, along with close friends, a married couple and their six-month-old son. The room we were using as a temporary lounge was going to have to become the second bedroom. So we had some urgent rearranging, along with the purchase of another double bed.

Allowing ourselves a day off, we visited the big shopping mall on the outskirts of Périgueux. We had been told by Denny that there was a huge second-hand store on the site which was worth trying. Sure enough the store contained a fantastic assortment of furniture, including enormous bedroom suites with eight-foot high double wardrobes. Several heavy ornate French sideboards were for sale - they would have taken at least four men to lift. We noticed a pair of tall, solid oak second-hand doors; useful in the future when looking for French patio doors to make a rear entrance to the cottage. We took careful measurements.

We settled on a solid medium oak bedhead and end section with side bars, in very good condition, which was not as large or heavy as others on offer and more in keeping with our cottage. Lastly we purchased the slatted base required to support a new mattress, both on sale in another shop. The bed frame was transported in the back of the estate car, with the base and mattress strapped on the roof.

Back at the cottage we considered the measurements of the set of oak doors we had seen. Each door had a 55 cm square wood panel at the bottom, with twelve small individual panes of glass in a slim moulded oak frame. Although over two metres high the width of the two doors together only measured 120 centimetres. Placed in the centre of the back wall there would be adequate space left either side of the room. As the height of the proposed lounge was three metres, it needed a high doorway in proportion to the room and the existing tall window.

We definitely did not want to put in a modern style patio sliding door. These original French doors were perfect for the look we wanted to create. The alternative would be bespoke doors, made by a carpenter to exact specifications. The doors were on sale at 38 euros for the pair, an absolute gift.

The next day we returned with the trailer to collect them. We would have to store them somewhere for a long time as the back-door entry was a low priority, but an essential item had been crossed off the 'materials to purchase' list.

We worked hard in our remaining weeks. At last the dining room and kitchen area had been wallpapered. The two windows from these areas were taken off their rising butt hinges (luckily this system makes them easy to remove) and worked on outside. The old paintwork was stripped, sanded and then repainted. The dining room table was taken out of wrappers, along with the solid pine Welsh dresser. Both items had been stored since being brought over on the trailer eighteen months previously.

Finally the dust sheets covering the dining room floor were taken up, revealing the newly-varnished floor. A few self-framed souvenir prints, obtained from a visit to the Musée d'Orsay in Paris and seeming appropriate in a French cottage, were hung on the walls. Ornaments were placed around the new oak shelf running around the room. It was all coming together on the ground floor. The new bed was assembled, turning the temporary lounge into bedroom.

I was concerned about the top of the staircase as there was no balustrade, just open stairway entering the loft area. Our son agreed to bring over a baby gate to seal off the foot of the stairs for safety reasons. But at least there was a working kitchen with safe electric plugs everywhere. They had two double bedrooms to accommodate them and four cottage-style chairs scattered about the dining room for the evening. Luckily the weather would be good enough for them all to make plenty of use of the space outside.

Just before we left, the farmer arrived with his tractor and cutter to mow our acre; he then returned the next day with a different attachment fixed to the tractor. This enabled all the grass cuttings to be shaken about, allowing maximum drying in the sunshine. There are pickings to be had in a recently-cut field. Often the kites and hawks will circle and pounce on unsuspecting mice, voles and sometimes snakes, now exposed amid the strewn straw, along with the many magpies and rooks that constantly turn it over.

The farmer returned on the third day with a baling machine behind his tractor which collected up a portion of the hay, encircled it with a tight strap and coughed out a large bale of hay. It was fascinating to watch. Our acre and the adjoining two acres belonging to the neighbour opposite produce eighteen large bales. In the evening he arrived with a hay wagon, yet again with another attachment to his tractor, and loaded them onto the cart. What a sight his modern green and yellow tractor made pulling the loaded hay-wagon out of our field something I will never forget. These bales would be taken back to his farm for storage as winter feed for the cattle which grazed around us.

We had enjoyed a super three and a half months; hard work but lots of lovely memories, eating evening meals outside and spending warm sunny days in the garden regarding the scenery. In early spring we heard the cuckoos, their distinct sound constantly echoing in the surrounding woodland. We had watched the many animals around us, deer, lizards, mice, black carpenter bees and numerous varieties of wild birds, not to mention the snakes.

On warm evenings we had taken walks along our hamlet. During one of these evening strolls, just as the sun was sinking, we had a brief encounter with a wild boar. It was after the farmer had cut the hay, leaving it strewn over the meadow. Approaching our cottage with the hamlet behind us, we could see in the hazy distance what appeared to be a large black dog. As we got closer the outline became more like a pig. The animal ambled across an open field from the large wooded copse on our right, and as it crossed the road its outline was clearly defined. It then wandered onto our acre, entering over the culvert which covered the ditch. It thrust its snout into the cut hay, tossing it over, perhaps following a scent.

We stopped, holding back and not wishing to get too close, as these animals are dangerous. I think it got our scent as it then quickly trotted across our acre up to the forest on the left of the road, disappearing into dense foliage; it was now safe in his own habitat. It is very unusual to see them out of the woods in the daytime, but it was dusk. Often we see evidence of their hooves and snout digging around our walnut trees where they have ventured at night. Perhaps on that late spring evening he was out courting, looking for a female in pastures new.

So to date, after our first long visit in retirement, we had no regrets for the restoration plan - roll on the next visit.

At last it was September and we could return again. We had spent a very hot summer in England. The whole year was turning out to beat all records for sunshine. The trailer had been carefully stacked again, including the new French patio doors purchased at the second-hand store. During the summer they had been stripped back to the original oak, removing some very dark shellac paint, and restained medium oak. We were loaded up with more wood and tools that could remain permanently.

Our son and his friends had really enjoyed their stay. Their note of thanks left on the table included the request "please book us in for next year". By way of thanks they had fully stocked the wine rack.

Evidently, according to my neighbour, they had spent much of their time at the cottage, not venturing far. Every evening they had a barbecue in the garden. On three days they had visited the man-made beaches at the local lakes nearby. At dusk they would promenade along the various walks.

We don't usually see cows on our acre, but when we returned that autumn there was electric fencing running along our boundary between our meadow and the neighbour's adjoining meadow. In her area was a very old-looking bull and alongside him a cow. My neighbour said it was for companionship, although I was not quite sure what she meant by this explanation. Either he had a special duty to perform with this cow or she was there to keep him company as he was nearing the end of his days. We shall never know.

A few days later marching along the road outside out cottage we saw the farmer's wife, Madame Sautet, and two cow-hands with six cows. The cows, suddenly seeing the bull, charged straight into our front garden trying to get into the field but were prevented by the electric fence. The cow-hands now had the job of trying to herd these animals back to the road. No such luck. The cows were now running amuck all over our acre, avoiding the lads quite easily. The more they chased them the more excited they became. It was obvious it could turn into quite a dangerous situation, as these beasts were very large and could easily knock the lads over.

Now our concern turned to the small saplings we had spent so much time and trouble planting. The cows kept venturing near the boundary edge and we thought any minute one of them would trample on these frail two-foot high conifers.

Eventually one lad managed to grab one of the cows, which he led out of our acre on the far side, and gradually the other cows followed. They marched them back the way they had come, the cows having forgotten the reason for charging into our field. All we could think was that they had recognised the bull and wanted to join him. We were relieved that our small trees had been spared. We have never seen the cows marched down the road again from that day to this.

As the weather was dry and settled we put up new fascia boards at the front, side and back of the cottage. It made a big improvement and covered the bare wood left by the new roof replacement. While the weather remained dry, Ray took the chance to paint all the new wood with white undercoat and top-coat.

Work on the fireplace commenced. There was to be a backdrop of bricks forming a small fireplace behind the new wood burning stove. We had gradually built up a supply of bricks on trailer pulls. The bricks were antique in design and looked like they had been there for years; we used dark grouting to create the right image.

Behind the stove area, supported on the bricks, we placed a thick oak mantelshelf in wood we had found in an area over the workshop. The old oak, which showed evidence of woodworm, was planed, stained and finished off with three coats of varnish.

The reclaimed match-boarding brought from England was fitted from the mantel shelf up to ceiling height, stained dark oak to match the colour of the staircase and finished with varnish. It all looked very pleasing and provided an excellent backdrop for the new stove. Looking as though it had been there for years, it made a nice feature in the corner of the dining room.

To complete the picture we now had to bring the log burner from the workshop. Being too heavy to carry, it was dismantled; luckily the door and top came off easily. It was reassembled on the newly-built white stone plinth. This stood out against the old red quarry tiles which had been uncovered when removing the old kitchen units.

We then measured for the lengths of black pipe "tayou" required to take the fumes up to the ceiling height. Our new pipe would meet the existing three-metre flue which was already in situ in the loft area ending at chimney height on the roof. A day spent actively searching for all the necessary pipes, joints and adhesion materials seemed a success. We returned exhausted, only to find that another connection was necessary between the pipe and the back of the stove. It took us several trips everywhere to find the right size of pipe and various connections to make the new log-burning stove safe to light and to make it comply with all safety regulations for our own benefit.

Barbecues were a must most evenings; afterwards it was lovely to enjoy walks along the village and surrounding countryside. The brambles we had cut back last June round the walnut trees had begun to grow again, but by keeping the grass short we were holding them at bay.

We decided to plant two more walnut trees where it was evident that one had been removed in the past. Not easy, as these new saplings had to be constantly watered in the hot weather. We had to walk about four hundred yards across the meadow, taking buckets of water down to the site by wheelbarrow. By the time we reached the trees we had lost most of the water.

Another chore was to water the 55 small conifers, which were suffering from the summer heat. Most of them had survived, but one or two would have to be replaced.

At harvest time, when there were signs that the shucks of the walnuts were cracking, we were able to spread our plastic sheet under the walnut trees and, with aid of a long pole, shake down the nuts. It was much easier now the grass was regularly cut around the trees. Gathering them up in wheelbarrows, we would then sit and remove the shells, wash the nuts and lay them out to dry. We placed them in cardboard boxes and empty food trays obtained from the supermarket; they were left in the sunshine each day to dry out, and we would return them to the workshop at night. After about ten days of this they were considered dry enough. This was the first year we had been able to do a full harvest; the yield was about forty kilograms.

On our return that summer we had observed the notices posted all around the lanes and one on our fence, 'Réservé pour la chasse'. The neighbour indicated it was to do with the hunting season. Sure enough, one misty morning early in October we were hearing shots from the forest. Ray was working in the garden when suddenly he saw about six men, shotguns on their shoulders, hound dogs sniffing alongside them, marching across our acre. They continued to march across the road into the farmer's field opposite. Quite a shock to us; with no 'by your leave' they can just march all over your property. But apparently the notices give them the right to hunt across your land; that is the law. We are used to it now and it does not worry us.

A few days later we could hear quite a commotion going on a hundred yards up the road on the edge of the copse. Quite a few shots rang out, really loud shots, followed by lots of shouting and dog barking. Then Madame Sautet, the farmer's wife, came along on her bicycle. I was in the garden and she stopped. "Beau temps" she said pointing to the sky, indicating the good weather. I pointed to the forest and looked puzzled.

"Un sanglier, un gros sanglier" she said. "Il est mort. Très grand, très, très grand. Deux jours!"

She was telling me they had shot a very large wild boar after chasing it for two days. These animals can be dangerous, which is why it is best to stay out of the forests at certain times, especially in the hunting season. We had seen men posted around the edge of the forests with shotguns ready, waiting in a stationary position for ages as the men inside the dense foliage are flushing out the prey. The white vans they used to follow the hunt around from forest to forest were now collecting up the dogs and dispersing. It had been a successful day.

In October Brian and Judy arrived back in Ribérac. Invited to lunch, we enjoyed sitting by their newly-installed swimming pool. It looked lovely, and they had been working hard to finish the surrounding area, laying slabs and reinstating the garden. Deciding we all deserved a reward for all the work we were undertaking in our projects, we treated ourselves to an evening meal in an expensive restaurant at Aubeterre. That evening, after enjoying a delicious meal, we were warned by the English-speaking French chef that the temperature was expected to drop that night to minus six degrees. Sure enough the next morning looked like it had snowed. What a picture; a beautiful crisp morning, then warming up to a glorious sunny day. This happened for three consecutive days.

We were now busy each day in the garden, clearing up before the winter months. We did the annual knuckling back of the two front trees; we also found time to take down the laurel tree at the side of the cottage. This gained us plenty of ground around the side area and allowed much more light into the kitchen.

The recent cutting of verges and ditch clearing (carried out by the local Mairie) had resulted in a splendid job. It meant the ditch along the side of the house in the white lane was accessible. Now we could tackle the privet hedge. We had three enormous bonfires in the middle of the acre with all the debris, including the laurel tree. What a burn up! We thought it would never end, but the bonfires easily consumed it all, leaving just a small mountain of grey ash. Just in time, towards the middle of November the rains started. It would have been far too wet for bonfires then.

The electricity went off about mid-morning. Usually it

pops back on within the hour, if not sooner. After an hour I went to find my neighbour in case it was just our property. No, it had been a serious cut, "une grave situation" and it would be a while yet.

The evening came and still no power. We managed by the aid of a small primus for the kettle and had salad for dinner. Next morning we went off to find a generator. We travelled for miles, but the shops had sold every last one.

On returning home I was now concerned about the freezer full of provisions. After speaking with Marie-Odette she arranged with her neighbour for my contents to be split between their deep freezers to save the food. She explained that the farmer would come round with his generator and top up the deep-freezes to keep them going. I was very grateful, as after twenty-four hours the food was beginning to defrost. We had lost the bread and ice cream. At least the supply of meat, which included precious duck breasts, had been saved, along with the home-made cakes. When evening came the novelty of candle light was wearing off.

That day, during our search for a generator, we purchased a dual ring which ran on a gas container; this enabled us to cook a hot meal. The cut had lasted three days, finally ending amid loud cheers only to go off again after an hour. But then it was finally fixed, much to the relief of everyone. Needless to say we managed to get ourselves a generator when the shops got restocked. It is quite essential to own when these electricity cuts occur. It is the overhead cables that cause the most problems, although on this occasion it was a serious major break which had put the whole area out within a fifteen-mile radius for three days. Even Judy and Brian, just outside Ribérac, had been without power for three days.

During the last couple of weeks we made a start in the loft area. The first job was to sand the beams. At present they were very rough and hairy; we wanted them to be nice and smooth. After distressing they would remain proud of the plasterboard ceiling and coloured dark oak. It was quite a nasty job, dust everywhere. They had stained up really well. It was going to give a fantastic backdrop to the rooms upstairs. We obtained an enormous can of beam varnish from the bricolage; this sealed them and enhanced them with a satin finish.

Prior to sanding we had covered up the open area over the top of the staircase with plywood and dust sheets. Entry was made difficult as we had to carefully manoeuvre in and out of the sheets; although tedious this stopped all the dust falling to the newly-decorated area downstairs. We decided to leave this area permanently covered. It made life awkward, but it did help to keep the heat in the downstairs rooms; the idea proved successful, containing most of the dust we were continuously making upstairs.

We moved any remaining left-over sheets of plasterboard from the workshop up into the loft. Plasterboard does not like the damp, so this would ensure it stayed dry. Next job in the spring was to line out the end walls; wood for the fixings and a plastic damp-proof membrane had already been purchased.

During the last week of our stay our neighbour Marie-Odette

invited us over for an evening meal. She had relatives staying; her brother Philip and his wife Sophie. We were wined and dined in the full French fashion. She served us home-made soup and then her own foie gras. The main course was leg of venison. The hunting season (la chasse), which is from late September through to early November, had resulted in a deer being shot in the forest. This forest was some distance behind her property, to which she had rights. The law of the hunt (in our region anyway) is that some of the animal is given to the owner of the land.

The meat had been marinated for twenty-four hours and then slowly roasted, and it was delicious. This was followed by two more courses. What a meal! And to accompany the meal, wine from St Emilion. Our conversation to the host was through Sophie, who translated from English to French and vice versa, enabling us to find out about the area, its history and the inhabitants of the hamlet.

The last few days were spent shutting up the house for winter. Plastic covers were put over all the mattresses and bedding stored away in the cupboards. Humidity containers in each room would help absorb damp during the winter months. The trailer was loaded with the walnuts and, as usual, cases of wine for ourselves and obligatory orders for relatives.

So on a damp late November morning we pulled out of our hamlet to return to England. On the journey we summarized the year's efforts. For the time being we had finished on the ground floor, now having our open-plan kitchen and dining room with exposed beams (although Ray often likened them to a Dorset tea room).

Our efforts during the first year of full-time retirement had definitely produced a leap forward. The next stage would be continuing progress with the loft conversion.

Time to explore

We took the ferry from Portsmouth on Tuesday 24th February 2004 on a chilly but very calm evening. It was a smooth crossing for winter. After a hearty breakfast we embarked to a sunny but cold morning. We enjoyed a good journey following our usual route, arriving at approximately 5 pm. Everything was as we had left it last November and there was no evidence of mice, plumbing leaks or major problems. The house felt cold, but once we started getting things unpacked we did not notice. By 7.30 pm we felt ready for our meal and went to our usual haunt in Aubeterre.

Next morning we awoke to warm storage heaters inside, but a very cold morning outside. A couple of days were spent getting the curtains up and rooms back to normal. On the Friday we visited Ribérac to get stocked up, and while we were shopping it started snowing. Small flakes fell at first, but by the time we returned to the cottage it was snowing heavily. Snow in the south of France – we were not expecting this!

The cottage looked very pretty covered in the white stuff and so did the surrounding countryside. Just as in England, it all seems to go very quiet when everything is covered in snow. I went outside to take lots of pictures. By 4 pm the snow had all melted in the sunshine.

Indoors it still felt very cold, even with the heaters on. Nothing for it but to test the log burner and light up. Great! What warmth. Although it was only a small stove the heat quickly spread through the cottage. It stayed cold over the weekend, but there was no more snow. First thing Monday we were making a serious start in the loft.

The new water heater was situated at the top of the stairway. The newly installed electric cables ran along the sides; these would be hidden from view when the dwarf side walls were built. The beams that were being kept exposed had already been sanded, stained and varnished. A small area of beam was left where we had run out of stain. That was my initial job while Ray made a start on preparing the end wall.

The priority was to begin work on the wall at the far end (front of the cottage), creating a new bedroom. This end wall would be lined with plastic sheeting, insulated and then covered in plasterboard. So on Monday we made an early start.

We do not get many visitors. When there is a knock on the front door it is usually the neighbour, so when I opened the door early one morning to see a uniform it took me by surprise. The middle-aged man did not do the customary "bonjouring". Stern-faced, he was pouring out a load of French, completely alien to my ears. I finally established that he was from the EDF, the electricity company, and he had just taken a meter reading from the compteur situated up a pole in the corner of the garden.

He was getting annoyed. I was looking completely blank and making no conversation that would appease him. Finally, using his fingers, he was imitating a pair of scissors. At last, realisation - he was going to cut us off!

I rushed to get the cheque book. No, that was no good; he could not take the cheque. He pointed to the address on a letter head. "Vous devez faire une visite à la bureau" he said. As best we could, we assured him we would go immediately, that very day. He turned his back and walked towards the gate, still imitating a pair of scissors.

Finishing our breakfast, we studied the address on the letter-head, a local office in Ribérac. We hoped their office was open and it was not a public holiday or we fancied we would be cut off by the end of the day. Goodness knows how much they charge for reconnection.

In the office, the man behind the counter was a little more sympathetic. We had been paying the account by direct debit every two months as is the custom in France, with a hefty standing order charge. Having now been at the property on longer stays we had not increased the amount to cover the electricity we had been using. The bill, only being read annually, had escalated, and we now owed a huge amount of money, over 600 euros. We settled by cheque, assuring him that the direct debit would be amended to take account of us staying for five months a year. Oh to be blessed with the gift of speaking the French language! If only you could have a chip inserted into your brain and French could come fluently from your mouth.

The delivery of 22 sheets of plasterboard, along with other materials, was on time. We carefully carried each sheet into the workshop, covering it with plastic to stop any damp. These boards were then cut into smaller sizes, as and when required, to enable us to get them up the stairs.

After I had finished staining and varnishing the beams I assisted Ray in cutting plasterboard. The far end wall was lined with a strong plastic membrane, using wooden battens to hold it in place. Because there was not enough ceiling height to use full eight-foot sheets of plasterboard, we cut each sheet to size. We put a strong wood centre fixing about four feet up from the floor, to which we fixed the lower plasterboards. Then we cut the top sections according to the slope of the ceiling.

The width of the new bedroom was determined by the thick existing side beams which joined the beams supporting the roof. These two sets of side beams divided the loft area into three sections. Because these beams could not be removed we had to incorporate them into the new dividing walls. Ray had to build the partition wall around these. He used 3" x 3" wood to extend out from the side beams across the room. He had to strategically place supports so the plasterboard could be attached at four-foot widths. The doorway was in the centre of the new partition. Again the large central beam running the length of the loft determined where the doorframe was fixed.

Once the dividing wall had been erected across the room, this gave the outline of the bedroom; three metres in width from the end wall by seven metres across. We could now think about installing the ceiling. The installation of the new roof had provided a felt lining underneath the tiles. We now intended to fill the spaces between the rafters with insulation.

On our shopping day in Ribérac we came very close to the purchase of a French car. Passing the Peugeot garage, we spotted a lovely red 406 on the forecourt. Stopping to inspect we found it in good condition, although like all the cars we had seen it had done a lot of mileage. We were taken for a trial run and Ray was very taken with the fact that it was left-hand drive, making for safer driving on the French roads. After discussion the salesman would not budge from the price of 5,000 euros, required in cash. We agreed to these terms and told him we would return the following week after arranging for funds to be transferred into our bank.

The next few days were frantic, visiting banks arranging for transfers and finally an appointment with the bank manager to obtain our 5,000 euros in cash. The morning we were due to visit the showroom I had come down with a terrible cold and it took me all the effort in the world to join Ray to collect this car. We arrived at the showroom as arranged, clutching the briefcase full of cash. We could not actually see the red car and assumed it was ready for us round the back.

"Bonjour, comment allez vous?" he said. He did speak a little English, so we continued.

"We have come for the car."

"I have some bad news for you. It is sold."

"We have the money" I said, indicating to the brief case, "we have collected it from the bank".

"You have the money?" His eyes opened wide.

"Yes 5,000 euros, what we agreed" we replied.

He looked surprised, as if he had not expected us to turn up, let alone get the money. Probably his experience of the English is they let people down, do not turn up on time or not at all. So he must have had another offer which he trusted more.

"It is sold, sorry". With that he shrugged his shoulders and disappeared back inside.

We were completely deflated, to put it mildly. After all our efforts in obtaining the cash it seemed unbelievable. We returned home really disappointed; it had been a very attractive-looking car. Over the past months we had spent a lot of time travelling miles to Peugeot showrooms in our region, which were few and far between. I think that was the final straw and what decided us to give up on the idea of purchasing a French car and stick to our idea of leaving our estate car in France.

Outside in the garden I had been busy cleaning and cutting the old glass fibre which had been saved. I opened each roll, spreading it out over the driveway. I cleaned off the old dead wasps and insects and then cut it to an exact size to fit in between the rafters. Finally the plasterboard was cut into widths for the pieces to join in the middle of the rafter, thereby giving a wooden fixing for the screws.

We had now been at the cottage about three weeks. We had previously agreed with close friends in England who had recently invested in property in Alicante to take some time out to visit them in Spain. We drove south through France, crossing into Spain and followed the coastal motorway to our destination. The husband had been experiencing serious health problems and the diagnosis was not good, so we felt it important to keep our promise; they were a few years younger than us and not yet retired, and we had known them for twenty years. They could only do short visits to their property in Spain as they ran a business. They were very keen for us to see their new venture, which they were so proud of. Like us, they had expectations to spend more time in their second home.

We set off, followed the route south towards the Pyrenees. Crossing into Spain we found a hotel for the night, then continued our journey on the Saturday. It was quite a long drive to their property. We spent a couple of days seeing their recently-acquired house and surrounding area. Unlike ours it was brand new, completely finished and very comfortable. The weather in Spain was warmer than France. We sat outside for meals and visited the local beach a couple of times, where we enjoyed the warm spring sunshine and ate ice creams. Then we made the long journey back through Spain, hugging the coast road and then crossing into France, where we stopped for a night at a hotel at the foot of the Pyrenees.

We then returned to our daily routine of working on the ceiling. Slowly, metre by metre, it was getting covered. Like some giant jigsaw, each piece fitted into its pre-determined space. The boarding was taken from the central exposed beam at the highest point of the ceiling sloping to the next exposed beam. From this lower beam it continued to slope to the edge of the cottage, which was actually the floor level of the loft. We completed the ceiling over the bedroom end and the area in the mezzanine, but the area over the stairway and the proposed bathroom had yet to be finished.

The side walls would be set back into the room a good metre. By coming in this distance it gave the room a more sensible side height of five feet. The very small sloping area the other side of the partition to the outer wall of the cottage would be useful storage space. Our intention was to build a small low entrance door in the walk-in wardrobe to enter this space.

On the opposite side wall in the bedroom we intended to use the low space to install a double set of chests of drawers. Thereby we could keep as much free floor space in the bedroom as possible. Once the ceiling was finished we could start making these supports for the side walls. The material for the side walls was plasterboard lined with fifteen centimetres of polystyrene.

Arrangements had been put in place with close family to celebrate our ruby wedding anniversary at the beginning of April. They were going to travel to France to celebrate the event. A new airline route had opened from Bristol Airport flying to the small airport at Bergerac. They arrived lunchtime on a Friday; our intention was to spend the weekend in Bordeaux. Paul and Sally, along with our daughter and several suitcases, all packed into the estate car and we set off for Bordeaux, where we had a reservation in a central hotel. From a previous visit, we knew of a very nice restaurant offering an excellent menu. Lucky we had booked, as they were turning customers away. There was a great menu including steak and fish, all cooked on an open wood fire which greatly enhanced the flavour.

Saturday was spent in Bordeaux enjoying its many attractions. There was a large open-air market to visit in the morning in the St Michael quarter. Adjacent to the market was a very old four-storey building full of antiques. We enjoyed wandering around the different floors experiencing the history of France through the various ancient objects, pictures, furniture and books. In the afternoon we spent our time in the many large, posh shops near the opera house, mingling with the French shoppers.

The new tram network was being undertaken at this time and new electric rails were being installed in the roadway ready for the trams. It was quite an achievement to keep traffic and pedestrians moving as normal around central Bordeaux while getting this mammoth project in place. New platforms were also being constructed, complete with ticket machines, at each of the proposed stops along the route. We promised ourselves a return trip in the future to ride on this very modern streamline transport.

That evening a taxi was arranged to take us out of Bordeaux. The venue was a nightclub on the outskirts of town, for dinner and entertainment. We celebrated in style with a lovely meal followed by an excellent show. This was compered by a very talented male singer who suddenly burst into a jaw-dropping operatic performance. There were showgirls in exotic costumes, and several variety acts. As the whole evening was totally spoken in French the comedian lost us, but everyone in the audience was thoroughly enjoying the jokes. Lastly we could all finish the evening on the dance floor. I think all the family were surprised at the quality of the show; we felt confident it would be up to expectations, having seen a quite a few live shows in France (Paris and Toulouse) and they were always tip top.

Sunday we planned to return the family to Bergerac airport, but first we visited the small village of Saint Emilion. It is very picturesque, with lots of cafés and small restaurants. Here we enjoyed lunch, followed by a walk through the small shop-lined streets winding upwards. These shops sell very expensive local wines and tempting food products of the region. Stopping for *dégustation* (wine tasting) at several shops and then purchasing souvenirs, our route ended at a château hotel with a magnificent view overlooking the surrounding vineyards and beautiful countryside.

There was no intention of taking the family to see the cottage as the visit was purely to celebrate our anniversary. Paul and Sally would be visiting later in the summer and my daughter was planning a trip to see us the following month.

After saying our goodbyes we returned to the cottage and we continued our daily routine fixing plasterboard. It was more of the same - day in, day out. We would carry the plasterboard upstairs, cut it to size and fix. The work was interspersed with weekends that would allow us some free time after the household chores. One Sunday, during free time, I had cleared the ground at the side of the cottage to prepare it for laying plastic sheeting and stones. We decided to lay black plastic sheeting to stop weeds returning through the stones. Now we had to find a supplier for the stones.

Saturday 17th April was the day we had been invited to

Marie-Odette's 70th birthday party. The whole hamlet was invited. We duly arrived for apéritifs at midday and one by one we were introduced to the inhabitants of our village. There were sixteen people to sit at the long table which had been arranged in her large lounge area. It was a bit daunting at first not being able to converse and not really knowing anybody, but fortunately we had been placed between her daughter and partner visiting from Brussels, who both spoke fluent English. Opposite was Sophie, who explained all the different courses.

We started with a traditional soup dish, followed by home-made foie gras served with salad. Special wine accompanied this, a 1988 Sauternes. Then Sophie's *pièce de résistance*, a speciality fish platter accompanied by *gratin dauphinois*, which was out of this world. Then the *plat principale* (main course) – fillet of beef, cut up into individual portions served from a large plate passed round the table. The wine was Pomerol, which, by this time, was flowing freely.

The guests, who had known each other for most of their lives, chatted and laughed and Sophie interpreted some of their jokes and memories as the meal progressed. Then we were offered the cheeseboard, again served with complementary wines. The dessert was a specially-made gateau from the local pâtisserie, accompanied by a sweet dessert wine.

There was discussion about the quality and taste of the *cépage* (variety of the wine) but this conversation, although interpreted very well to us by the host's daughter, was fascinating but superfluous knowledge. We have gradually learned about the wine regions and can only now appreciate the French people's deep understanding of wine, especially living so close to Bordeaux. It really was a privilege for us to attend this celebration and meet our French neighbours. In total it had consisted of six courses, each course having been prepared and presented faultlessly. What a splendid feast. It had started at midday and finished at 5.45.

During the meal Sophie had explained to a lady in the village who worked at a local firm supplying commercial materials for road building that we needed stones for our garden. She told us to visit her cottage that evening and she would place an order for the stones. In fact she was the same person who had arranged for the supply of earth to repair the crater in our front lawn a few years before.

By the end of April we were beginning to enjoy more settled weather. We had decided to take a break from the loft area and try to get the wall on the front of the cottage tidied up. We had brought over our water compressor to remove the layer of dirt which covered the Tyrolean finish.

Covering ourselves against the spray, we began hosing down the wall with the compressor. Using our triple folding ladder, which we opened to form a platform, we placed a scaffold plank across the top to balance on. By this method we were able to reach most of the wall. The remaining area under the eaves was reached by a ladder on top of the scaffold plank. Ray sanded down the old original pale blue paint which had been under the eaves. After undercoating he finished off the whole area in a white gloss top coat.

In the trailer we had brought over three 10-litre tubs of masonry paint; a lovely rich creamy colour. These were quite heavy. We had calculated that we needed six tubs to paint all outside walls of the cottage.

Once the cleaning was finished we chose a fine dry day to start the painting. We intended to do an undercoat, thinning the paint for this, then the following day put on a thick top coat. We started very early - we wanted to complete each coat during one day as we did not want it drying out patchy.

The undercoat went on quite well as it had been thinned. The texture of the render on the wall was very rough; this made the work very tiring on the arms. It was a much larger area to cover than we had realised and by the end of the day we felt exhausted. We took the following day off to rest our arms. Then the next day we tackled the final coat. We started early, but by the middle of the day the sun was moving round to the front of the cottage and was on our backs as we painted. Again we had to move the scaffolding along, balancing ladders on the plank. The temperature in the shade was 26 degrees; in the full heat of the day we were absolutely burning up, but determined to finish the task. As we were using the paint at full thickness it was very hard to spread on the rough render. We only just had enough paint to finish the two coats, having used the full three tubs. Our calculations for six tubs were way out. The reason why the calculations did not match the manufacturer's guide lines was the roughness of the render.

Because of the weight of these tubs we had to gradually bring the rest of this paint in our next two trailer trips. On completion of painting the outside walls of the cottage we had used twelve 10-litre tubs.

Our plan for the following spring was to paint the north side of the cottage and the following September the south side. We knew from previous experience of painting a house with masonry paint that it was very strenuous work, so we decided to do it in three stages. At the rear of the cottage was the workshop and outbuilding. Until we had decided about the rear doorway we would not get involved in painting this area.

The front was completed, making a huge improvement. To finish off we painted the stone surrounds of the windows in white masonry paint and likewise the stone edges of the cottage.

We were now in the middle of May, and our daughter was due to stay for a week's holiday. She was flying to Bergerac from Bristol; her last visit to the cottage had been in September 2001 when she had helped us by painting emulsion on the bathroom walls.

She was quite amazed to see how much work had been done in the two and a half years since her last visit. Although she had seen the pictures and videos of our progress, it is still more realistic actually being in the house. Whereas on her last visit we had a makeshift table in the old kitchen area, she could now sit at the large table in the new dining room and appreciate the cottage-style atmosphere we had created, along with the new kitchen area. She was keen to see how much progress had been going on in the loft area and was surprised to see our efforts with the new walls and ceiling in the bedroom area.

Caroline accompanied us to the local markets at Ribérac and Chalais and we managed a few sight-seeing trips to various places. We ate our evening meal outside most evenings, enjoying the very warm weather.

One night I put the black rubbish bag outside the front door on the porch step, intending in the morning to take it to the waste bins in the middle of the hamlet. Next day the bag was slightly open and the rabbit bones, which had been secured inside a white pedal-bin liner bag, had been removed (without tearing either bag) and picked clean. These were now left on the step.

"Now there's a mystery" I said to Ray. "What could have done that? Not a bird for sure, and a fox would have torn the bag".

Later that morning Ray called out to me, "I have found the culprit. It's asleep in the barn". By the time I went outside to see it had gone.

"It was a kitten" said Ray.

"Where's it gone?" I asked.

"She or he ran off as soon as it saw me".

The three of us were sitting outside at lunchtime looking down the garden towards the shed when a little face and paw peeped out from under the aviary area. It was the colour of ivory with a tri-coloured tail and darker shaded paws and tipped ears. Where had this little kitten come from?

Ray took a tiny dish of milk down and we waited. After a short while the little cat ventured out and drank. We repeated this later with a dish of some salmon left over from lunch, and the kitten immediately smelt the fish and came straight to the dish. It dived in, warily looking back at us all watching. But it was hungry enough to overcome its fear. By the evening we had refilled the dish with some pâté and now it let Ray stroke it. Originally we thought it might be a kitten from a feral cat which had been killed, but from its behaviour we were becoming convinced it was domesticated.

That evening we ate outside; the kitten came to the table and started to rub around our legs, purring constantly. Evidently very happy at our company, it was jumping up onto Caroline's lap, where it seemed to want to sleep. It was a very pretty with enormous light blue eyes set in a sweet face. There was no question - we would keep it.

The following day we bought some cat food, returning to find it asleep on a comfortable chair close to the house. It seemed to be making itself at home with us. A decision was made to take a photograph and post it on the notice-board in our hamlet by the rubbish bins. Surely someone would be missing this pretty little kitten? Though perhaps, on the other hand, it could have been dumped from a passing car by someone not wanting to keep a litter of kittens. Perhaps a person returning to England had just turned it out after their stay.

On the way to the notice-board I saw Yvette, the lady in the hamlet who kept a ménagerie of animals opposite her house along with sheep, goats and geese in a penned area two hundred metres up the white lane. She was definitely known in our village as a connoisseur where animals are concerned.

She agreed to come and see the kitten and expressed how attractive it was. Most French people in a rural area keep a cat for mousing. Yvette sexed the kitten, deciding it was definitely *femelle*, and said she would be happy to take it.

But after making extensive enquiries all around the area, no one knew of the kitten, or its mother. So she is now the property of Yvette, who instantly took to her. After her precarious start in life she is now a very lucky cat indeed.

I would dearly have loved to have kept her had our circumstances been different. But one drawback to our dual life-style between England and France is that pets are not allowed on the agenda.

We kept the grass cut around the walnut trees, a monotonous chore but one which would prove beneficial in gathering the harvest in autumn. It was also very therapeutic. Once down in the area around the walnut trees you were at the edge of the farmer's crops, with cows grazing in fields opposite. The tall grass and wild flowers from our meadow and adjoining field would sway in the breeze; red kites circled high in the blue sky above us, occasionally returning to their nests in tall poplar trees in the adjacent field.

As the season progressed you could smell the aroma from the growing walnuts. Our cottage could now be viewed from a different aspect, far away in the distance alongside the roadway through the village. The small, strong building stood proud amid the ample gardens, and while we were enjoying our time spent down at the boundary edge we would often look towards the house, contemplating how unbelievable it was that we could own all the land between us and the house.

Our delivery of thirty metric tonnes of stones duly arrived, three deliveries of ten tonnes each on a small lorry. This gave the driver a chance to back up close to the area for the drop. Two loads were spread along the side area where I had managed to cut back the ivy and weeds to widen the footpath. The last load was for the front. All these stones were laid onto the black plastic which, hopefully, would stop the weeds returning. It had made such a difference tidying up the ground around the cottage; with the front wall now freshly painted it showed off the restored green shutters.

During May we had taken a weekend off to visit the seaside resort of Royan. We wanted to check out a hotel. It had boasted individual villas in the garden with a pool and footpaths leading to a lovely sandy beach. We booked ourselves in for a week in July. We were keen to try the new air route from Bristol ourselves. We planned to hire a car from Bergerac and drive to Royan.

We returned to England in late May and in early July we flew to our holiday in Royan. The new air route seemed to be taking off with lots of passengers. Our villa was very pleasant; it was situated in the gardens of the hotel, where we accessed Nauzan beach. Around us were several other different beaches to enjoy. The main town of Royan boasted many chic shops and the choice of restaurants was amazing. The most enjoyable feature was the coastal walk. It stretched for miles, a continuous path perfectly protected, with safety rails along the more dangerous cliff edges.

One day of our holiday was allocated to visiting the

cottage to cut the grass. It was roughly three hours' drive from Royan. It had been a fairly wet summer; on arrival the grass was very long since the last cut in May. It was a good job we did, otherwise it would have entailed a long strimming job in September.

Sadly, on our return from holiday we were met by the news of our friend's death. We were so pleased we had seen him during the promised trip to Spain. His health had quickly deteriorated over the last few months and although we had seen him in England on our return before visiting Royan, we had not expected that he would die so soon.

Last March, his dearest wish had been to return to Spain for two weeks during the summer. Life cannot be taken for granted. If you are lucky enough to have the chance to fulfil your hopes, then make the dream come true. Seize the opportunity and don't look back. It seemed so unfair to us. Why our dear friend? He had an amazing personality with an incorrigible sense of humour that could make everyone split their sides with laughter. He was greatly missed by so many other friends and colleagues. We often talk about him and will never forget him, a truly lovely guy.

We spent July and August in England, getting together the materials for our return trip to France at the end of August. We were expecting two visitors from Australia in early September. Ray's family had emigrated a year before we got married and his parents had taken their four other siblings to Adelaide. His eldest sister Ann had married Ian, an Australian, shortly after we had married in England. In the early years of their lives in Australia it was not affordable to visit England. Eventually, as cheaper flights became possible between the two countries Ann was able to return to England several times, first holidaying with Ray's mum, then with her twin sisters and finally with her husband and their two boys.

This year Ann and Ian were planning a trip to England. Interested to learn of our plans with the cottage, they intended to include a stay with us in France. We had warned them that it was still in a very basic state; although we had two bedrooms we still did not have any rooms upstairs.

We met them at Heathrow Airport at the start of August and they stayed with us for a few days before touring Devon, Cornwall and Yorkshire. They would fly to France after touring England, spending a week sightseeing in Paris. Our plan was to travel to France by ferry at the beginning of September. We would then meet Ann and Ian at Angouleme station after they had travelled by the TGV from Paris.

On our return in early September we found the grass quite dried out, brown and sparse, although thankfully it was not too long, having been cut on our visit from Royan, but everywhere was overgrown with foliage and weeds due to heavy rain in July and early August. The large climbing rose on the north side had got so large that the support wire had not held, and it was draped across the sideway.

The next few days were spent 'opening up'. We cut the lawns around the walnut trees and pulled out the enormous weeds growing in the driveway. The weather stayed extremely hot and dry and the temperature had reached 38 degrees in the shade by Sunday, so we had to stop any work by early afternoon. Monsieur Raynaud cut our meadow and returned to bale up the hay on the Wednesday.

We were due to pick up Ann and Ian from Angoulême on Thursday at 1 pm. The weather was still very hot and dry but a more comfortable 27 degrees. We set off early to visit the Géant to check out the purchase of two relaxing garden chairs. Up to now we had not had the luxury of lazing about in recliners, but we thought our visitors might appreciate the chance to do so.

We arrived at the station in good time. It was quite exciting to see the extremely smart *Train à Grande Vitesse* arriving on time. Our relatives alighted, pulling heavy suitcases and enthusing about the very smart train on which they had just travelled from Paris.

We were a bit apprehensive about Ann and Ian's visit as the cottage was still fairly basic, especially with the installation work that was going on in the loft. But after collecting them and driving back to the cottage they were soon appreciating the lovely scenery. As we all sat in the garden drinking wine and Ian a cool beer, they said they were quite amazed with our countryside views and peaceful village.

We had arranged a trip for them into the heart of the Dordogne to visit medieval villages, and give them a flavour of France. We had reserved rooms in the hotel at Monpazier where we had stayed the previous year on our wedding anniversary. We then drove them to Sarlat, spending a day in this magical town. Following this we visited Beynac village, built up a steep hillside, which involved a very arduous climb.

It culminated at the magnificent XIIIth century Beynac feudal castle, once occupied by the Barony of Périgord. This castle is perched high on the hillside with views over the Dordogne valley. It is beautifully preserved; work is continually undertaken to keep the building and surrounding walls restored and preserved for history. At the same time it is a great tourist attraction. Although most of the rooms are empty, the feeling in the castle is extraordinary. As you explore the castle the ambiance suggests that at any moment people of the twelfth and thirteenth century might suddenly appear. The lower entrance takes you into an open courtyard area within the thick walls. Here is the drawbridge where horses would have galloped to enter the castle. You tread the ancient uneven stone steps from the kitchen area up to various levels, through large banqueting rooms, intricate hidden passages and more stairways leading upwards. Eventually you exit into the fresh air surrounded by turrets overlooking the fabulous Dordogne valley. It is one of the best castles I have ever visited.

Lastly, on our two day excursion, we managed to check out some other beauty spots along the Dordogne River, observing the many canoes and kayaks which are always a popular sport in the shallow waters.

Our friends Brian and Judy were back at their cottage along with four guests from Bristol. On Sunday we took Ann and Ian over to meet them and swim in their pool. We arranged a return visit; they would come over to us for lunch the following day.

Monday morning was the *marché* in Chalais. Personally, we think it better than Ribérac market as all the traders' stalls are spread along the roads throughout the town itself and the main road is closed to cars. The market culminates in a large area at the end of the route where they sell live chickens, ducks, geese and other poultry. Ann and Ian were quite taken with this market. We collected fresh fruit and vegetables, returning to prepare the lunch for our visitors. It had been a lovely sunny morning but had clouded over at lunchtime; we thought it best to lay the table up inside.

Our six guests arrived and we managed to sit ten around our table, enjoying a ploughman's-style lunch accompanied by French bread and fancy pastries from the boulangerie-pâtisserie in Chalais. Then outside the sun shone through the clouds and we went into the garden to enjoy some friendly conversation along with the wine.

The following morning we were up very early to take Ann and Ian to Angoulême to catch their train back to Paris, where they would catch their return flight to Australia. We were so pleased that they had been able to visit the cottage. They praised our efforts and wished us success in finishing the work upstairs, promising to return to see the cottage completed. They could not express enough compliments about the scenery and their short visit into the heart of the Dordogne countryside. They had only been able to spare five days, but luckily, we had been able to cram a lot into their visit. We felt quite pleased, but surprised, that they had thought so much of our small cottage.

We continued working upstairs. The bedroom end had

been completed only in as much as it had a ceiling and four walls. The doorways had yet to be built with the surrounding framework. The next job was the side walls for the middle area of the loft. Again the lower supporting beams, which joined the roof beams, were gradually covered with supports and plasterboard so as to form an internal wall between the mezzanine area and the new bathroom. Gradually over the next few weeks the loft began to take on a new look.

On the 1st October we began to harvest walnuts. It looked like it was going to be a bumper crop this year. We shucked them and laid them out to dry each day in the sunshine, and after weighing we had fifty kilos.

One day, while collecting this harvest, we saw European cranes flying south-west to winter in a warmer climate. Their loud calling sounds first alerted us to look upwards and see hundreds of them flying over in long V-shaped columns. If we are lucky enough, we also see them in early springtime flying north-east. Sometimes I see them when talking in the garden with my neighbour Marie-Odette. We stop to watch, fascinated as they swoop and dive high overhead calling to each other "C'est une autre signe de printemps", she says - yet another sign of springtime.

The following day, a Saturday, we visited the river Charente, looking for slipways. Ray had been looking into the possibility of accessing the waterways near to us. A navigation book we had purchased showed many navigable areas along the river. Planning our route, we arrived at Sireuil, a small town which had a fleet of hire boats. Arriving at 10 am we were aware that there was a gathering of people. A ribbon was strewn across a brand new slipway giving access to the canal. It was obvious some sort of occasion was about to happen. We mingled with the crowd and then the mayor and various other dignitaries arrived. We had actually stumbled on the official opening of the new slipway.

The Maire did a speech and from what I could gather he was praising the success of the tourist industry in the Charente region and saying this new slipway would encourage more people to use the waterways. Our future plans included the possibility of obtaining a small trail boat which we could keep in France to use on the rivers. In the past, when holidaying in France, we had hired small cabin cruisers and experienced the beautiful and peaceful scenery on the waterways. We could not really believe we had actually chosen that very morning to pick out that little town, at random from the map, to coincide with a brand new slipway being opened.

After the opening we toured the area alongside both sides of the river. We established that many of the small pretty towns such as St Simeux, Jarnac, Vibrac and the main central town of Châteauneuf-sur-Charente had ample moorings and facilities for boating. The scenery around that area was picturesque with tall, leafy trees along the towpaths and open fields with wheat crops.

By 18th October the nights were beginning to turn a little chilly and we had started switching on the storage heaters. As Marie-Odette had been poorly, I offered to help with the annual foie gras bottling. Sophie and Philip were visiting and as in most years Sophie and Marie-Odette had purchased twelve ducks to prepare for the festivities of *Noel* (Christmas). The liver of the duck is carefully prepared and canned into little tins and slowly cooked to make the precious foie gras. Then the legs are bottled into the famous *confit* (preserved cooked duck legs) and all the remainder is made into *grillons*, a form of pâté.

As we sat in the kitchen I was trying my hardest to speak French, with Sophie correcting me. It was fascinating to see how they followed this routine, the customary preparation for the winter season. The whole procedure had taken two days. First the preparation, then cooking and bottling. Finally the tins containing the foie gras are taken to a local hardware store, where a special machine seals them. The tins are labelled and kept for a couple of years to improve the flavour.

On Friday 22nd October we were invited over to Marie-Odette's for evening diner along with Sophie and Philip. We enjoyed a lovely meal following a similar menu to that of the birthday party. We have since learned that our region of Périgord is blessed with some of the finest produce of France. The locals have, over the centuries, enjoyed the most envied recipes throughout the world.

Just as we were expressing our thanks for the lovely evening Sophie presented us with a hand-painted picture of our cottage. We did not realise it was one of her hobbies and that she often exhibits paintings in her small home town in Normandy.

In the last week in October we visited Belves to see the Marché des Noix, the walnut market. I had read about this market in one of my books on the Dordogne and decided that as we were now walnut farmers ourselves, we would investigate. We arrived quite early and found the centre of the town deserted. At about 9 am the first small white van arrived; a farmer alighted taking out two 45-50 kilo sacks of walnuts. Then gradually other vans arrived with their sacks. This gathering of walnut farmers constituted men and women of various ages. Many were elderly couples who had probably been bringing their small crops of nuts over the years, others younger men with quite large harvests. Some produced a single sack, others as many as ten. The ancient covered market square was filling with sack upon sack of walnuts. People greeted each other and became involved in lengthy conversations, probably discussions on whether they had been able to dry out their nuts due to recent rains. Numbers grew and grew.

Eventually a large white van arrived and the driver emerged and started moving from person to person, inspecting their bags of walnuts. The bag would be opened and he would crush one or two in his hand. After consideration he gave the person a paper ticket. This was the price he had agreed to pay per kilo for their nuts. After he had inspected all the bags he returned to his van to get out the large set of scales. One by one they brought their bags over to be weighed and exchanged the nuts for the value on their ticket.

We do not know what payment had been offered to the

sellers. The ticket prices varied; if walnuts are not dried out properly their shells can look mouldy. Obviously size is important. Lovely large walnuts, perfectly dried, would fetch more in value. We had considered perhaps in the future that this might be a way of disposing of our walnuts. At present we return them to England and through a local source sell them in our local farmers' market. We had customers who were desperate to obtain our French walnuts; containing more oil, they are not as dry and bitter as the ones from California or various other countries of import.

We had one week left to pack up the house. Curtains came down and were put away in the oak wardrobe. The rugs were rolled up and mattresses covered in strong plastic to protect them from humidity. Electricity and water were turned off and the tank drained down. We had a visit from Marie-Odette, who kindly offered to keep a watch on the property. I am sure that if she saw any strangers hanging around she would report it. Likewise if any problems occurred due to storms she said she would let us know via Sophie, who would telephone us in England.

On a dark November morning our car, pulling the trailer loaded with walnuts and wine, left the small hamlet in thick mist. It remained foggy for most of the journey. We arrived at Caen, where we were booked into a hotel close to the quayside. The early morning crossing was scheduled to arrive at Portsmouth midday.

Unfortunately we were delayed five hours outside Portsmouth harbour, due to a crane falling onto a ship; the MoD had prevented all boats from entering the dock.

Eventually we arrived back in Bristol at 9 pm. We were not best pleased as we had to peel and freeze two kilograms of large prawns which we had brought back from France for Christmas menus. Thankfully, we retired to bed at midnight.

CHAPTER TEN

Travels with my aunt, and some French lessons

When we returned in the spring of 2005, we knew we would need a lot of motivation to continue with the repetitive work upstairs. Encouraged by seeing the progress made on the two previous visits last year, we were tempted to finish the bedroom and have one room complete, but resisted. We decided it was more important to get all the partition walls in place.

Fresh deliveries of boarding arrived; this batch included the special vapour resistant panels essential for bathrooms or any room where there is high humidity. Over the years, since our first order and including the special thick dwarf walling sheets, a total of 66 sheets were installed, along with boxes and boxes of plasterboard screws.

One of my contributions to the whole adventure was the title of 'project manager', which involved knowing exactly what materials we had in stock, keeping a complete record of supplies and an up-to-date cost for the project. I had to ensure we had enough funds regularly sent over to our French bank account to keep up with the purchases we were forever making.

The hardest area to tackle was over the stairway. With no floor to support ladders – just open air - we had to seriously consider how we would balance ourselves to install a ceiling and board-off the sides.

At present the floorboards ended at the edge of the open stairway. Scaffold planks were placed across from each side edge. Using our triple ladder as a platform placed on the scaffold planks, we gained sufficient height to reach the ceiling. It was very daunting looking down over empty space to ground floor level. It was no problem for Ray working in this area, but I felt more comfortable crawling out along the platform before standing upright.

The Velux window over the stairway had to be encased in wood before it was joined to the new ceiling, there being a depth of approximately twenty centimetres the depth of the insulation between the roof felt and the new ceiling.

Sticking to the original plan, we finally completed all the partition walls, including the thickly-insulated dwarf side walls in the mezzanine and in the bathroom area. We followed the same design as the bedroom, leaving plenty of space behind.

Now we could turn our attention to completing the bathroom area. To allow enough room for a full length bath, the position of the bathroom wall opposite the top of the stairs was very critical. Careful measurements decided where the new wall would be positioned. Wood supports for the partition between the bathroom and the landing area were erected up to the width of the bath, then stepped back, encroaching into the bathroom area to allow enough walkway on the landing.

The doorway was proving difficult. In order to open into the bathroom, the door had to lose a top corner to fit the slope of the ceiling. By chance, we had kept a door from our present house in England; opaque glass in an oak frame. This proved to be an excellent idea. Combined with a window of opaque glass, built high in the bathroom partition wall, it gave maximum light to the landing.

Our intention was to use the bath from downstairs. I know, after all the work in that small bathroom we were now going to dismantle it! But we had no reason for two baths in the cottage.

We continued working on the new partition wall and doorway, which seemed to take longer than anticipated as the measurements were so critical. Gradually it took shape and Ray could think about installing the new low-level coupled toilet and cistern.

The large wash-basin had to come forward on a purpose-built casing. This was to keep full head height while standing at the basin to clear the slope of the ceiling. All the copper pipework had previously been installed. The sewerage and waste pipes from the bath and sink then had to be coupled to the outlet pipes, which we had installed before we built the back wall. Luckily, installing a small trap door as at the bedroom end meant we could go through behind the side wall to do all the coupling at quite a reasonable height.

In early April we decided on a break away for a couple of nights in Bordeaux and a chance to see how they had progressed with the new tram network. We caught the early train from Chalais to Bordeaux and boarded one of the new trams to the central shopping area. These comfortable streamlined carriages operated by electricity and were quiet and smooth, effortlessly transporting people around the city of Bordeaux and out to the suburbs.

The fixed amount of one euro fifty cents (purchased on the platform from a ticket machine before embarking) covered a single journey, or a daily ticket cost four euros. Astounding, they had built this network of tramways on existing roads while keeping the city's traffic system operating. The trams are powered by APS (alimentation par sol) - ground power. The powered rails are on the road surface with the electrical power collected by skates located under the tramcar. There is no problem with pedestrians walking on these rails, which only become live when the tram passed over them. Ingenious.

We envied the French transport system; their high speed trains were comfortable and reliable, along with a good network of regional trains. These new tram systems are available in several other cities. The city of Nice was shortly to complete installation of their system.

We enjoyed our short break, a pleasant day out away from the monotonous regime of plasterboarding. We explored the shops, visited an art museum and had lunch at St Michael's

Passage, an area full of antiques. Our train at 17.00 departed on time, returning us to continue our never-ending mammoth task in the loft.

The weather was now settled, with lovely warm, sunny days, and we decided to continue with the plan for painting the cottage. The north side was next on the agenda, which included the area around the front door. The original door, which had been sadly neglected, was removed and sanded back to the bare wood for treatment and restoration.

The wrought-iron hand rails around the front steps and under the porch canopy were stripped of their peeling black paint and exposed rust, then treated with special Hammerite black paint. The area around the front door and along the north side was undercoated with the cream masonry paint and then finished with a thick top coat. Under the eaves the wood was painted white. Around the large windowsills and the pretty brick surrounds we painted in white masonry as a contrast to the cream. We completed this work in about two weeks of hard effort, the weather holding out for us. The south side of the cottage was scheduled for the following year.

In May we expected a visitor – my aunt from East Yorkshire. Luckily an airline had opened a new route from East Midlands to Bergerac airport and on a bright and breezy day we collected her from the airport. Aunt Margie had always loved travelling to new venues, and continued undertaking these visits with my uncle until his death in 2001. She had a keen interest in historical towns and buildings, expressing genuine pleasure wherever she took her holidays. The next week was spent visiting interesting places, which included a day out to St Jean-de-Cole, a delightfully picturesque village full of pretty, ancient cottages either side of a wide traffic-free road. Luckily, on the Sunday we chose to visit the annual festival of flowers was in full swing. Stalls lined the avenue, spilling onto the green leading down to the river Cole.

Aunty had known all about our plans for the cottage, having seen the original photos taken in 2000. We had visited her in Yorkshire a few days before we left to do the purchase with the vendors. She was very interested to see for herself how much progress had been made in the last five years. Although appreciating the amount of work left to do, she praised our endeavours so far, promising to return next year.

After Aunty's departure we were now approaching the middle of May and had only another couple of weeks before our return to England. Our son and his friends intended to visit in the summer. Wisely, we did not endeavour to move the bath. This would be left until our September visit.

Back in England we went hunting for a small trail boat that we could take over to leave permanently in France, to use on the river Charente. Our searches finally led us to a small boatyard in the village of Laughton, near Lewes, East Sussex. There we found a sixteen-foot Bonwitco glass fibre boat with solid mahogany edging and a small top cuddy. This cuddy, while not high or large enough for sleeping, did have a seating area and storage for luggage taken on a day trip. There was a single narrow seat across the centre.

The boat was in fairly good condition for a life of twenty-five years. Evidently it had only been used on rivers. It was not considered sea going as the side height from the deck was quite low. It was for sale complete with a trailer (which had seen better days), but after discussion a price was agreed which included a spare trailer wheel and a boat manoeuvring jack.

The seating arrangement would need to be changed, with the removal of the centre seat to provide side seats and build storage cupboards underneath. A mature oak floor was planned and refurbishment was needed on the original mahogany guard trim. With staining and varnishing this would be returned to its former glory. As there was no power, a new outboard motor was needed.

Within a couple of hours the seller had made the old trailer roadworthy, adding tailboard lights, and we hitched our new-found purchase behind the estate car and set off back to Bristol. It was backed onto our driveway, where it would stay until the renovation work could begin over the next few months. We planned to take the boat over the following year, 2006, in September.

In September we returned to France. After a very hot and dry summer at the cottage we had lost several of our small conifer trees. The grass was very brown and everywhere looked very dry. Our son had been impressed with our efforts above stairs and could see the outline of rooms emerging.

Hornets are like giant wasps. You are warned about them and told "don't on any account interfere with their nests". Brian had discovered a nest up his chimney and had tried unsuccessfully, with assistance from Denny, to get rid of it.

On the second attempt it was finally removed, only to have it return again the following year. Hornets, which can be extremely large and intimidating, had frequently flown through the many gaps in the loft area before the installation of the new roof. You can't mistake the drone of a hornet; its sound is very deep, different to a large bee.

Our son, over with his friends in the height of the summer, had encountered a hornet's nest. The empty bird box on the pear tree, close to our cottage, previously had a family of great tits that spring; closely watched by us they had duly left, along with four fledglings. The box, being empty during our absence, was long enough for the hornets to take over occupancy and build their nest.

Paul noticed many hornets flying around and mentioned it when Madame Moyrand came over with produce from her garden. She spotted where they were coming from and said she would return. Meanwhile he remembered the can of spray in the workshop for killing hornets. Scantily dressed in shorts and flip flops, he sprayed the contents into the box. The neighbour returned in her beekeeper's outfit. She had the proper hat to protect the face with all the netting, and a blouse-like jacket along with gloves; she was fully prepared to tackle the nest with her can of spray.

I could imagine the scene, a sweltering hot day, and suddenly Marie-Odette, quite a short lady, appearing round the side of the cottage completely covered in protective clothing. A scene from a Ghostbusters movie descending on the watching audience, who, I imagine, were all trying hard to keep straight faces and probably thinking it was an over-reaction on her part.

She told them they were lucky that the spray had been successful and that the hornets had not headed out of the box; it could have turned into a dangerous situation. A few hornets were returning, but luckily the liquid had killed the nest. Later that year we dismantled the box. Sure enough a fully-developed nest was inside. No way near as large as the nests usually created inside lofts, these having to be removed professionally by experts.

The advert read "French teacher seeks extra pupils for French". On telephoning it appeared my French was too basic, as her pupils were advanced students. However, she took my number; it appeared she had been contacted by other English people requesting help. She agreed to form an hourly lesson once a week. It was with a little anxiety I attended the first class.

There were four of us in the class. Fred, as he introduced himself, was in his late fifties and had left England with his wife, selling a smallholding to follow his dream - a home in France. It seemed as though he had swallowed a French dictionary as he knew loads of vocabulary, but like me, he did not understand how to link it all together using the French verbs which change everything. The French verb *venir*, meaning 'to come' is just an example. For years I had said to my French neighbour "Je venir prochain septembre", But what I was actually saying was "I to come next September".

During our first class Fred informed us he had lived in France a year but would dearly love to talk in depth with his neighbour, his conversation being limited to two topics, the garden and weather. The other two members were a couple just arrived in France; they were renting until they decided on an area to settle. The husband, John, knew very little French and it was evident he was going to struggle. His wife Miranda had a basic knowledge from school lessons. So after introductions our teacher, a confident young French mother, proposed we tell her the areas where we needed help!

Although our lessons proved a little fruitful, one hour a week was far from perfect. Each week we attended faithfully, making notes to follow up at home, but at a cost of twenty euros an hour it was proving quite expensive, especially for the couple. The lessons did not follow a strict pattern, jumping out from one area to another where we requested help. The most helpful element for me was her advice to purchase *Le Nouveau Bescherelle*, a complete guide to conjugating 12,000 French verbs.

So at last I had some available reference to verbs, which furthered my need to understand how they change in gender, spelling and pronunciation in all the tenses, past, present and future, this not having been explained in my French conversation classes in England.

At the end of autumn we returned to England; with a total of ten lessons under my belt I felt keen to keep up my studies. During that winter the teacher obtained a full-time permanent position, so her small rented studio closed, along with our chance of further knowledge of the language.

By chance, the following spring I was put in contact with a lady in a village close to us. She was English and worked part-time at Périgueux College, teaching English to senior students. Although she confessed to not being fluent, her French was very good. My 'saviour' (as I call her) did not hold formal lessons. Because her circle of English friends had all expressed their desperation with the language she decided that on one day a week she would hold an hour-long class in her home. Whereas my previous teacher did not seem to follow a strict format, my English lady, Pru, was more exacting. She would insist on the right pronunciation at all times and the correct gender for all words.

The lessons were great fun, as each week a variety of people would turn up to sit in on the group. I was making friends with these ex-pats, all at varying ages and each with a contrasting reason for leaving England. Pru would choose a different subject each week and then after the lesson, in her own time, make a CD recording to give us the following week. This allowed us to play it over and over so we could practise the correct sound of the French. My French came on leaps and bounds with her help. She would not take money for her lessons as she was helping her close friends.

It was fun to see the retired couple from Liverpool with their broad accent improving every week as we talked in basic French describing our backgrounds, hobbies and reasons that had brought us to France. The homework was to bring a written diary of what we had done during the week and read it out in French. One young mother, Emily, had come to France with a tiny baby, now with three boys two of which were at school, she was at last getting to grips with the language; overcoming her fear of talking to the teachers on parents' evenings. But however hard she tried, she could not lose the broad Birmingham accent which shone through her French pronunciation.

We had always been fascinated by the cottage in our hameau with the number 74 above the front door. Knowing our house had connections to the railway, which had run through our hamlet, we endeavoured to find out more. Enquiring of our French neighbours, we were told of the steam train that took them to Ribérac. I felt sure that a trip to the local library might impart some history on this railway.

Saint Aulaye had a *bibliothèque*, a small library, which had recently been refurbished. I remembered seeing this building during my visits to the town. One Friday afternoon, finding it open, I searched among the various sections until I came across the perfect book - *La Ligne du Chemin de Fer* (The Line of the Railway) written by Monsieur Jean-Jacques Beauvais. It appeared that the author was a local historian, and had been written within the last ten years.

Obviously the book was in French, but it was well punctuated with pictures and diagrams. It commenced with the establishment of the railway from Paris into the south west of France. It listed the people who had pushed for the steam train to be extended into the rural areas, along with the dates of each successive opening of new routes and stations. Our local line had commenced at Périgueux and was constructed to Ribérac by 1881. Then it was extended through our area to Parcoul–Médillac by 1906.

Local stations were named and illustrated, with

occupants who had posed for photographs at various dates. It explained how the construction had been undertaken with local labour. I found it quite absorbing and very informative. At the end of the book it gave the email address of the author.

I was very anxious to purchase a copy of this book, as eventually I would have to return the borrowed copy back to the library. The author replied instantly to my email, informing me he had some spare copies. He lived within ten kilometres and gave me a date to visit him, along with directions to find his house. It transpired he was a local historian and was busy completing his latest book, dedicated to the village of Aubeterre.

Monsieur Beauvais was more than happy to answer our questions on the local railway line. Also he provided a photocopy of the original route, which passed within metres of our cottage. We explained we were trying to establish if our cottage had been linked in some way to the railway company.

Comments had been made that our cottage was built solid and sturdy "like a railway property" and as we had discovered various rail connectors and other railway items on our land we thought it likely that there were definite connections to the railway. He explained that the house in our hameau with 74 above the door was definitely a *maison de garde* and the number depicted the number of kilometres from Périgueux, the main terminus. The inhabitant of maison 74 would have been responsible for operating the level crossing. The nearest station had been Bonnes approximately half a kilometre away, but the train stopped at the level crossing to let passengers from our village alight, saving them the walk back from the station.

There had been sixteen maisons de garde built between Ribérac and Médillac, each alongside a level crossing. Like the maison 74 in our hameau, these houses provided habitation for railway staff undertaking to work the level crossing. Plenty of hand-drawn sketches illustrated the layout of each maison de garde and explained the method of construction, which was to a tight specification laid down by the railway company. From the diagrams they were indeed built very solidly.

Luckily he had copies available to purchase. It was a slightly later edition containing extra information since the original publication. It gave added details on the local *Résistance* movement during the war years and how the railway had played its part. This new section explained how the Résistance had blown up the railway to prevent the Germans invading. This had occurred in the Siorac de Ribérac, just outside Ribérac.

We have since been able to piece together a little more of the story of our cottage's origins. One Sunday we invited Marie-Odette over for lunch and during conversation (in the best French we could offer) discussed the railway history, showing her the book.

Our neighbour knew that during the early 1930s the resident of maison 74 had moved into our cottage. This was around the time our cottage had been built. Whether or not he had influence with certain builders and our cottage had been constructed along the lines of a railway building, we shall never know.

After lunch Marie-Odette took us for a walk, showing us

where the old rail tracks had been. It had run between us and our neighbours on the other side of the white lane. They now have the original level crossing and are using it as the gateway to their property. The track then crossed between maison 74 and Marie-Odette's property, running alongside and continuing through fields to Saint Aulaye. Now that I knew about the route it was easy to fathom the origins of the line in the contours of the surrounding land.

It would have been great to see the train steaming across the countryside; it would have been easily visible from our kitchen window, less than fifty metres away. The train would have travelled through the small villages, people alighting with their purchases from the market. The book gave the timetables for calling at the various destinations. There used to be three up and three down trains per day, with different timetables for the weekends. The book concluded with the demise of the local railway. In 1951 (about the same time as England was closing railway stations in small towns and villages) the trains were gradually replaced with autobus routes; these too have since disappeared as owning a motor car grew in popularity.

We have since explored the railway route by tracing it out on maps and visiting accessible spots, walking alongside the remains of tracks, although all the lines and sleepers are now gone. We have tracked down the original railway stations between Ribérac and Parcoul, which are all still intact, having now been converted into domestic homesteads.

Before returning to England the push was on to complete the bathroom. The plasterboard walls had been papered and the ceiling finished with textured paint before white emulsion. The wash-basin and toilet fitted into their allotted spaces with only inches to spare and all the copper pipes had been connected up. It only remained to remove the bath from the downstairs and install it in the tight fitting area upstairs.

After much struggling to negotiate it round tight corners and up the stairs and manoeuvre it through the doorway, it was finally installed between the wash-basin and end wall. The final connections were made by fixing the taps. It would have been much easier to place the bath when building the bathroom, but obviously we did not want to manage without the downstairs bath for that length of time.

We were now ready to commission the new bathroom. Ray had put stop taps on the hot and cold pipes leading from the water tank on the landing. The taps were opened and the water flowed in. There were a few minor leaks around the cistern, but nothing too dramatic after previous problems with waterworks in the cottage. It only needed extra tightening around various connections. The area around the bath and shower was tiled with 300 four-inch-square white tiles. We had brought these over from England, but unfortunately I had underestimated and a further hundred were required. Initially, under strict instructions from Ray, I began tiling along the bottom of the bath edge, but I was 2mm out of alignment and sadly, my tiles had to be removed before I was allowed to progress further. I think I have mentioned that Ray is a perfectionist!

Attention was then given to the annual walnut harvest and the tidying of the garden, always required at this time of year.

Our leaving date was fast approaching. It was the first week in November and we were packing up the house for the winter months. Next spring would see us back again to continue with the upstairs bedroom. Although the room itself was completed the doorway had to be finished and a door fitted; the walls needed papering and the floor varnishing. Inside the room another doorway had to be completed for entry to the walk-in wardrobe and fitting a double chest of drawers into the loft space behind the side wall under the window.

Once we had started using the bedroom upstairs, work could begin on the new lounge. This room, at present our bedroom, would be opened up with a new doorway to the garden. According to French building regulations it was necessary to obtain permission for any alterations which incorporated new windows or doorways. Ray had drawn up sketches and taken photos of the second-hand French doors we intended to use. This information was taken along to the local Mairie to obtain the permission; all the necessary official forms were completed and submitted, along with our drawings, to a central office in Périgueux. We could expect to wait some six months before any decision would be confirmed.

The return ferry crossing to France in February 2006 was going to be on the new flagship of Brittany Ferries, which had only recently joined the fleet. Our journey down to Portsmouth was ahead of snow which had been forecast for England. It was bitterly cold, so it was nice to get on board the new ship and enjoy an evening meal and a comfortable cabin for the night.

We arrived late afternoon and started getting some warmth into the cottage. Storage heaters were switched on and the log-burning stove lit. We made our usual visit to the café in Aubeterre for supper, returning in the cold night air, and it certainly felt cold.

After the customary opening of the cottage after the winter, which generally took us a few days to get up and running, we were back into the loft to continue. We could now use the bathroom upstairs. As we had brought the extra tiles from England, I completed tiling around the shower; by now I was quite a competent tiler, albeit slow. I made sure the tiles were perfectly aligned, especially on the first row!

Driving through the small village of St Quentin, on our way to Chalais market, we first saw signs along the roadside advertising "Banquet - Cochon de Lait" (feast of suckling pig) being held locally in the *Salle des Fêtes* (village hall). Every small town or village with a Mairie has its own Salle des Fêtes. This particular hamlet was privileged with a brand new one, built within the last year. While in Chalais we saw more posters for the event, giving a telephone number for reservations. It offered seven courses, apéritif, wine and tombola (lottery with prizes), all for the modest sum of twenty euros per person.

The date was a Sunday early in April. Arriving punctually at midday, we could see evidence of smoke from behind the new building. On the grassy area a shelter had been erected over the roasting spit; a large pig was already cooking. We parked opposite in the grounds of the massive church. Like many villages we have driven through around France, each has an enormous (and well-preserved) church. This very ancient, but recently restored, monument to Christ could easily accommodate two hundred people; strangely, there were only about two dozen homes in the hameau. You can't help but wonder why they built such large churches.

On entering the Salle des Fêtes we found ourselves in a spacious, tall, light and airy room. Our names were crossed off the list and a numbered ticket was given to indicate our seats. There were three long tables with place settings, wine glasses and decorations, each table seating around fifty people. A cluster of early guests were around the bar at the far end and we joined them for our apéritif. During the next hour guests continued to arrive. At 1.30 pm there was a drift to occupy the tables. As yet, we had not encountered anybody speaking English.

We had been placed opposite each other in the centre of the middle table. To my left was a party of five people, four women and one older man who was sitting next to Ray. He was communicating in French and Ray was responding (as best he could). Anyway they seemed to understand each other. Seated on my right was an elderly lady from a village in the Charente, an hour's drive away. Trying out my best endeavours with French I managed to ascertain that she was enthusing about the prospect of what was to come; it seemed to be a regular occasion on her calendar, one not to be missed.

Throughout the meal we were served by the organisers of the banquet, local people ranging from young teenagers to men and women in their seventies. Men were now placing bottles of red wine on the tables, one for every four guests, while still continuing to top up our apéritif glass with rose. The soup was now being served; ladled out from large soup terrines, it smelt tempting. Baskets of crusty sliced baguettes appeared all along the table.

The following course was an entrée of fish – *saumon et asperge pâté* (salmon and asparagus) accompanied with salad and crevettes. White wine was served during this course. Then a calvados sorbet was offered to refresh the mouth after the fish course. By now the guests were deeply immersed in the occasion and enjoying the companionship all around them and bantering with the *serveurs* (who were known to most of them). Pausing in the flow of the banquet, the raffle tickets were now being sold. The Charentaise lady on my right bought several books, not just one book like us – she definitely wanted to be in with a winning chance. "Les prix sont grands et très bon" she said (the prizes are large and very good).

It was now about three o'clock, and we had been there three hours and still two courses away from the main event, the suckling pig. The party on my left were getting really excited about the next course. It was locally-hunted venison made into a casserole dish with green haricot beans. We decided to pass on this course as we were already feeling full, and having drunk a lot of wine we decided to pace ourselves. After all, we really wanted to enjoy the roast pork. The French people were surprised that we declined the venison, expressing it as *surtout* (above all) and definitely the best course.

Finally around four o'clock large trays of sliced pork were being passed up and down the tables. It was delicious accompanied by bowls of small new potatoes and white haricot beans in a light-coloured sauce. The red wine we had consumed was now replaced with more expensive bottles. The labels showed it was from Bordeaux. We wished we had not drunk so much previously. The French were having no trouble consuming the new wine.

After the course of suckling pig the tables were cleared and the draw for the prizes commenced. The gamble by my neighbour paid off; she laid out her books of tickets exposing all the numbers and scooped three prizes - the last being a leg of wild boar to collect from the kitchen on her departure. Some of the prizes were consolation novelties to add humour to the occasion. I remember one *serveuse* winning a bright red and black underwear set. She immediately put the thong over her jeans and carried on wearing it for the rest of the event, laughing with her friends.

Then plates of individual brie cheese cut into quarters appeared, along with more crusty bread. This cheese tasted divine, so fresh and creamy. More wine flowed. Lastly we were served the dessert – individual pastries of *abricot, poire* or *pomme*. We made an observation that if this banquet had been in England, the situation would by now probably be quite raucous and definitely a few guests would be worse for the booze, but not at this function. People were still talking and laughing in the normal manner, with nobody behaving extra loud or annoyingly. The children had remained at the tables for most of the time; occasionally a few had wandered around but none had misbehaved.

Finally coffee was served, which we gratefully received, though we noticed quite a few people preferred to partake of the cognac that was being offered.

Making a supreme effort to stand, we bade our farewells to the people either side of us and express our thanks to the servers. It was now well past six o'clock and we finally made our exit from the hall along with other happy or merry guests.

Needless to say we were a little worse for wear the next morning! But it had been quite an experience to sit among the French people and participate in their social gathering; one of many events which are continually held in their small communes and always so well organised.

In April the small bathroom downstairs was made into a utility room. Ray placed the washing machine next to the hand-basin using the space that the top end of the bath had occupied. Opposite the washing machine we had sufficient space to move our small deep-freeze from under the stairs. This freed up space in the kitchen area, and it was great not to hear the washing machine spinning.

At last the doorway to the bedroom was finished and the door fitted. I had stained and varnished up the two original doors (one being for the walk-in wardrobe). The walk-in cupboard still needed to be lined out with plasterboard and equipped with hanging rails, a job for the September visit.

While Ray had been working on the bedroom doors, I had been painting all the skirting boards and varnishing up the floorboards. Lastly we papered out the room and then it was ready to move in. We decided to keep the move until after our return in September. There was still no balustrade around the landing area and the stairway was open. Luckily it was only our son staying during the summer this year; their friends were not coming as they were expecting another baby, so we were not so concerned about the danger.

The weather had now settled into a mini heat wave, and by midday it was far too hot to undertake any jobs. Keeping cool was the challenge; we would use the shade of the tree by the barn to relax under. On days like these, in the heat of the afternoon, the blue sky is completely cloudless, eternal over a landscape of shimmering fields. The air is heavy and every move an effort. You give in to the warmth and sit lazily in a lounger. Shade covers your head and there is a cool drink by your side. The book slips from your grasp as you finally succumb to the magic of "lazy, hazy summer days". What bliss! Even the birds have disappeared, seeking shade. No sound from the hamlet; the road is quiet and the shutters are all closed against the penetrating sunshine. Keeping rooms cool is a priority.

We returned home in early June. The plan for the next three months was to work on the boat which at present was sitting on our driveway. Since our experience in 2004 trying to purchase a reliable second-hand Peugeot car in France and finding they were more expensive and on average having driven over 200,000 kilometres, we gave up on the idea. During the summer of 2006 we bought ourselves a two-year-old Peugeot for use in England and decided to leave our fairly new estate car in France. It would prove useful for travelling around on holidays and pulling the trail boat.

As anticipated, the original mahogany edging along the sides and front of the boat came up like new after removing uneven traces of original varnish. It was then sanded and covered with three thin coats of boat varnish. Ray removed the seating and purchased some marine ply to make storage boxes. The original seating was solid oak, so it was sanded, stained and varnished and cut to fit into the sides of the boat over the new storage areas. The previous owner had steered from an outboard at the rear; we preferred to install an independent steering wheel with forward and reverse gears fitted from a newly-purchased outboard motor. Using ten centimetre thick foam I cut it to make the seating, covering it in a modern waterproof fabric. Various items such as fend-offs, a telescopic boating hook, paddles, towing rope and many minor accessories were stored in the boat. We then were ready to try it out on the river.

The next problem was to find a slipway from which the boat could be launched. We did not think living in Bristol with plenty of rivers nearby there would be any problem, but the nearby slips we found were either privately owned by boat clubs or deliberately blocked off, while a few were in a state of neglect. Eventually we travelled to Devizes, where we successfully made our entry into the river.

The maiden voyage proved a success, although it was not without problems. The most difficult task was to line the boat up to engage it back onto the trailer. We hoped we might improve our efforts with practice.

We managed to find a closer slipway for our second attempt. The Bristol harbour allowed us to enter our boat for a small fee and we made our way along the Feeder Canal up towards Hanham lock. This was a good day, taking our lunch and seeing the scenery of our city from a different perspective. But again on returning to the harbour it was very difficult to mount the boat onto the trailer.

After assistance from other boaters who had easily removed their 'ribs' from the river, we concluded that the trailer we had purchased was not the right length for the boat. We observed the modern trailers where boats were easily winched back with the assistance of rollers and decided to purchase a new trailer before we returned to France with the boat. This was managed just before our September trip. Although we did not have a chance to try it on water, the boat appeared more balanced seated on the new trailer. It made sense to have a reliable trailer before the long pull to our cottage.

As usual we had more building materials to take and luckily some lengthy items could be stored inside the boat. I remember we had to work out the pulling weight of the boat and trailer against the recommendations of the Peugeot handbook. We booked the ferry crossing; with the length of the boat the cost was the same as taking a caravan. Arriving at Portsmouth for the crossing we were placed on the lower deck and did not have to negotiate the ramps as we normally did with our trailer.

We had a successful journey, although fairly slow, pulling a sixteen-foot trail boat. It had been well strapped down to the trailer and several stops were made to check for any movement. Arriving in our village in the late evening, we carefully turned into our driveway over the narrow culvert with the ditches either side. Our French neighbours expressed surprise at the arrival of a boat in the small hamlet. We explained our plans to take it for day-trips to the nearby river Charente, about an hour's drive from us.

We did not have to wait too long to embark on our first trip to the river. The weather was warm and appeared settled. The previous day was spent preparing for an early start. We left at 8 am and arrived at Sireuil, a destination we had already visited, where we knew we could safely park and negotiate the reversing of the boat down the slip to the water's edge. Once it was in the water the boat gently floated off the rollers; the trailer and car were then safely parked on the nearby grassy area.

It was so beautiful along the river. The scenery along the river Charente was vivid and varied. It commenced with two large châteaux and then a small village. Leaving this behind it opened up into a large river with open fields of crops either side. Then, following our navigation guide, we had to keep left of the river for the first lock. The locks were not manned and it was fairly straightforward to work the large wheels, open up the lock and gain entry.

During our journey two locks were accomplished, then the river opened out; we cruised on under a large road bridge. We were at the small town of St Simeaux. Built along the bank was a special picnic area; wooden tables were awaiting us in a large well-tended grassy area. Tall trees swayed overhead, providing shade from the sun. It was a very pretty place to stop and enjoy lunch. The cool box in the cuddy had kept everything fresh, including the wine.

We then had to take account of the time and retrace our steps. As we cut through the water, only the sound of the outboard motor disturbed the peace. Now and then herons would come into view and take flight as we approached. We virtually had the river to ourselves, not much evidence of other boats; the occasional fisherman was spotted tucked in alongside the bank, we gave him a wide berth and a customary nod as we passed by.

The new trailer made it easier to negotiate the boat out of the river, evenly floating onto the rollers. The winch on the trailer easily dragged the boat from the water. Then, after using the car to pull it away from the slipway, the boat was securely strapped to the trailer before the journey home.

The sun was beginning to lower in the sky as we drove back across the Charente countryside. Open fields of golden wheat and maize crops changed to tidy acres of vines supporting the grapes ready for the coming *vendange* (grape harvest). The grapes would be used for the special Pineau crop - turned into wine and mixed with the famous Cognac (again, only produced in this region) to become the special apéritif drink Pineau des Charentes. Between our barn and the old bird aviary there was enough space to park the boat; eventually we planned to make a boat-port so it would be covered against the elements.

It was now nearly the end of September, and while we enjoyed good weather we took the opportunity to complete painting the south side of the cottage. The last of the old blue paint on the wood under the eaves was removed and protected with two coats of white. Then two coats of cream masonry paint finished the third side of the property. The back of the building was yet to be tackled; after the removal of the old 'cycle shed' outbuilding we would use the last remaining 10-litre tub to paint above the workshop and the area around the new doorway.

I do not dislike the small wall lizards we have all around us. Mostly we see them in the garden, but often a few are found in the house. In fact, now that I know they keep the spider population down I am very fond of them!

One good turn deserves another is my motto, and Ray certainly did this for our little friends one day. While he was painting the outside of the house one of these little creatures dropped into the paint. It was foundering and finding it impossible to get out of the pot, so Ray gently lifted the lizard up onto his hand. There he sat covered in thick creamy paint. He did not move but sat completely still, as if knowing he needed urgent help. Slowly Ray took him to the outside tap. There he carefully bathed him, washing off the thick coating. Gradually he was free of all the sticky covering and lowered to the ground. Then he headed off, with a quick look back as if to say thank you. They are inquisitive creatures though, not to be underestimated. They will eye you up and down even though we must appear giants to them. Often they fall through an open Velux window as they scamper over the roof. The best way to catch one is to put a shoe box over it, then cover it with the lid and tip them back outside.

On rainy days we continued to plasterboard the walk-in wardrobe and fit the hanging rail. We decided to paper it out and make the cupboards and shelving on our return in the spring, when we could work inside. We would now make use of the good weather to work outside on the annual garden tidying and walnut harvest.

At last, we moved into the new bedroom. It was great having drawers to put clothes in and a room to hang clothes. Up to now we had been using portable hanging rails and storing clothes in various places. As we slept in the new room, under the exposed heavy dark beams, it seemed our cottage was finally coming together.

We had managed to create a lot of character in the new loft area with the sloping ceilings and original wooden doors all stained up. The floor throughout the new area was now stripped pine and varnished. The area over the stairs looked very quaint with its wooden shelf and heavy character beams. Being upstairs in the cottage we often awoke to the sound of birds walking around on the roof. During heavy rain it was noisy on the roof and drummed against the Velux window but it was only a minor concern; the main achievement was that our new bedroom was so much cosier, with plenty of space for our possessions.

We had agreed to collect Judy and Brian from Bergerac and were well on our way to collect them when my mobile rang. It was Brian. "We have just been told to get off the plane, hope you haven't left yet?" he said. They had boarded the flight at Bristol and after a wait of twenty minutes the pilot had told them over the Tannoy, "Due to industrial action at Bergerac Airport the flight is cancelled. Very sorry folks but you must leave the plane, the company requests you book another flight."

Brian then informed us that passengers were using their modern mobiles to rebook for the next day; as he did not possess one he assumed any available seats would soon be taken by those who did. He described a dramatic situation with many people suddenly thrown into chaos. Couples and families sitting on board a plane out on the runway, geared up for take-off to a holiday destination, had suddenly realised that the holiday was cancelled. And then there was the hassle that would ensue at the other end for waiting relations and pre-booked taxis.

Brian, ever resourceful, told us he was heading home and transferring to his car. He hoped they would have enough time to make the Portsmouth ferryports for an overnight crossing. "If we make it I'll phone you tomorrow to revise our plans" he said.

We turned round and headed back home, surprised the airline could treat you like that. But it was just another case of the French suddenly downing tools because it suited them to protest.

Brian and Judy made the ferry and duly arrived the next day. Continuing our plans we visited their cottage, and met up with them again during the last week of their stay for an evening meal at the Château restaurant in Chalais.

According to the plan, we were returning to England on a flight from the nearest airport, which was Bergerac, direct to Bristol. Our estate car was going to be left in France permanently, so we had been preparing for this by filling out all the necessary paperwork to get it registered in France with new French number plates. This entailed the headlights being changed to conform to regulations, as the vehicle had temporary covers over the lights. The equivalent of the MOT was carried out and then we made the trip to Périgueux to the Prefecture (main city of a French department), where, frustratingly, we found one conformity form was missing. This had to be completed at our local Trésor de Public in Ribérac. On the second attempt everything was stamped and approved and we came away with our new registration number to enable us to get new French plates on the car.

The boat had been covered in black plastic and roped down against the winter elements. A car cover protected the car after we had disconnected the battery and left it safe in the barn. As for the walnut harvest, our two suitcases would contain as many of the nuts as we could manage for our customers in England.

Then on the news we learned of further threats of industrial action from the French air traffic controllers. By coincidence Brian's return ferry date coincided with our flight. One day prior to our flight we were notified by the airline on an email, "Cancelled due to strike action, refund or rebook". Thankfully, we were invited to hitch a lift with them to St Malo to embark on an evening ferry. This route was claimed to be the fast ferry, stopping at Guernsey and Jersey.

On board we were enjoying apéritifs and surveying the menu to enjoy a meal later. The ship had made its way out of the harbour and was gathering speed. Slowly we started to notice a decidedly heavy rolling, due to the enormous swell of the sea. We observed many people tucking into meals and not taking a lot of notice, but we soon found that trying to walk around the duty-free was impossible. We struggled to hold on to something to steady our balance as the ship lurched from side to side. Successfully back in our seats with our purchases, we sat tight. Luckily we had not eaten, deciding from experience that it is best to refrain from eating in this situation. It was going to be a long and eventful journey.

After a couple of hours it was quite evident those who had eaten, should not have. People were laid out on the floor, others tucking themselves in quiet corners in a bad way. The estimated journey of five hours turned out to be nearer seven. Eventually the torture ended and the safety of Poole Harbour was reached. Gratefully we made our exit from the port, Brian speeding us home for 2.30 am. We laugh about it now, but it was a journey we would all have rather not made.

CHAPTER ELEVEN

The end of the beginning

By 2006 we felt confident that the cottage would finally come together in the next year. At long last we could stop juggling rooms around between temporary lounges, storage areas and bedrooms. The new lounge would become a reality with an entrance to the garden. It was going to be a busy year, but hopefully, our most successful yet.

Unfortunately the new route by Flybe from Bristol to Bergerac ceased that winter. After two years, British Airways had decided to sell the route. Easyjet had taken over the route from Bristol to Bordeaux, but the flights did not begin until the end of March, and from Bordeaux Airport it was a much longer journey by taxi to our cottage.

When the Bristol to Bergerac route had opened in 2004 our friends Judy and Brian had brought a Renault Espace from England to use in France, leaving it at Bergerac airport on their departure. In those days Bergerac was just a small airport and the surrounding area was mostly grassy fields.

Parking was free and many cars were left at the airport for weeks. It was quite common to see lengthy grass around cars, obviously left for several months while their owners were out of the country. Judy and Brian used this plan and their Renault was left ready at Bergerac airport for them, family or friends for transport to their cottage. This was proving an excellent plan and one we intended to follow.

Meanwhile the airport had been growing, with new arrival and departure lounges in the process of development, so in 2006 the parking was no longer free. Large car parks had been provided for passengers and it would prove too expensive for us to leave our car at the airport for the months we were back in England. Although we were now in a position to use these cheap short-haul airlines, we had to add the cost of a rather expensive taxi fare to get us from the airport to our cottage. It was still a better option than the ferry, however. Their fares had been increasing over the years and an overnight cabin, fuel and road toll fees had made the journey more expensive. The biggest incentive was that the journey by plane could be done on the same day.

So in spring 2007 we had to make the journey from Southampton, the closest airport for us with a route to Bergerac airport; on arrival a taxi would be waiting to take us to our cottage.

It seemed strange not to be driving down with the trailer loaded with provisions and materials. Ample supplies of clothes had been building up over the years, ranging from a good selection of everyday working garments to smarter evening attire, along with plenty of shoes. Our two suitcases contained only essential items; medicines which would stock up our first-aid cabinet, along with a supply of personal items unobtainable in France. There were large boxes of tea bags and our three-kilo block of cheddar cheese. Also a small supply of tools for Ray; new masonry drill bits, replacement belts and discs for sanders, a new battery for his cordless driver and lastly a new saw blade. We gave the customary present - a kilo of cheddar along with large box of teabags - to our neighbour Marie-Odette. English tea bags are quite expensive in France and our neighbour enjoys the full flavour of a strong tea-bag, unlike the French varieties which are weaker.

We discussed the next and final large project, the rear entry to the property, and a decision was made to get professional help. Initially, Ray intended to cut the wall for the doorway and had even purchased the necessary cutting tool, but the existing cycle shed and outbuilding surrounding the area was made up of large stone blocks and underpinned with very heavy supporting beams. Although I was prepared to help, I did not think I would be able to assist in the removal of this structure. We decided to search for an English-speaking builder to explain exactly what we required. After cutting into the back wall, we required the builder to fit the second-hand French doors which we had purchased, remove the outside buildings and clear away all debris before erecting a new *abri* (shelter); these are usually designed with a tiled roof, supported by solid green oak beams and left open at the front and sides. This would give us a covered area right outside the new doorway to sit and eat meals al fresco. These covered shelters are very common in our area and are a great way to enjoy the outside, providing cool shade under the tiled roof, and escaping the need to clear the table in a case of a sudden, unpredictable Dordogne thunderstorm.

Three builders were selected from various advertisements. Two provided equally acceptable *devis* (an estimate of the work). Once accepted the price may not be changed; it is fixed by law and the contractor must abide by it. Another important factor in our decision would be the need to begin in early April and finish before our departure in early June. The second builder could not start for two months. We made our decision to go with the first builder and paid the customary thirty percent deposit, the final amount to be paid on completion. The French have quite strict laws on workmanship. The contractor must hold a SIRET number uniquely identifying his business, which means he is registered to work and pay his taxes. If you employ a builder working 'on the black' as the expression goes, you risk heavy fines or imprisonment yourself, so it is not a wise move to employ anyone without establishing that they have a SIRET number.

Jack, our builder, was a carpenter by trade. He had left England three years earlier, having run his own company there. He was now establishing himself in our area of France, building up his client base and undertaking most aspects of the building trade. After assessing our requirements he agreed to get the doorway cut and installed as a priority. This would enable us to use our time working on the new lounge while he continued to do the demolishing work and build the abri.

Since our move into the new bedroom upstairs the downstairs room (our previous bedroom) had been left completely empty in anticipation of work starting. The cut for the new doorway was carefully measured inside the room, it being critical to site the doorway in the centre of the outside back wall. From floor level inside the room there was a high drop to the ground inside the cycle shed which covered the back wall.

Jack began cutting into the solid stone blocks, which proved to be much thicker than anticipated and very resistant to his efforts. It took him two full days to complete the cut. The cutting tool Ray had initially purchased for the job was inferior. Even Jack's cutter did not work and only by attacking the mortar around the bricks was he able to inch them out bit by bit. So already we were more than thankful that we had decided to invest in professional help on this particular project.

While Jack was getting involved downstairs Ray was completing the installation of the protective balustrades and handrails along our landing on the first floor. These balustrade spindles had been hand-made by Mervyn, a friend of ours who, like Ray, is an avid do-it-yourselfer, specializing in woodwork skills. Using his woodturning lathe (a tool Ray did not possess) he created a reproduction of the existing spindles. Ray then set them into a handrail which matched the original staircase. I then undertook hand sanding and staining them dark oak, identical to the existing finish on the staircase. Finally two coats of varnish were applied.

Jack had now completed cutting the space for the

doorway. The wooden frame previously constructed in England by Ray was fitted by Jack. This covered up the exposed wall cavity; it was then made weatherproof with various compounds before fitting the French doors within the frame. Before he started the demolition work Jack covered the new doorway outside with a thick sheet of external chipboard for protection.

We could now begin our work in the new lounge, first removing the old varnish on the floorboards and belt-sanding them back to smooth wood. The old flock pink wallpaper was stripped from the walls, along with the old pink paint around the doorways. The tall windows had already been worked on last September when we had decorated the south external wall. These had been taken off their hinges and stripped of various layers of different coloured paints. Two panes of glass had been renewed and fresh putty applied to the glass. The solid oak surround around the fireplace, devoid of colour and varnish, was worked on to obtain a rich medium oak finish.

Because of the condition of the plaster the walls were not entirely smooth, so they were papered with a modern blown vinyl in a plain soft creamy yellow that had a texture mimicking natural walls. Matching all the paint work to the exactly the same colour as the wallpaper seemed to soften the room and blend it with the medium oak of the French doors and fireplace. After the final coat of varnish had dried on the floor we could install the furniture, which had been stored in the other rooms. The cottage suite and bureau found a permanent home at last. The new lounge now gave us a comfortable room for the evenings with instant access to outside.

Wasps are harmless enough when encountered in small numbers outside, but when you have a nest of them the size of a rugby ball inside your home you have a problem. Each day we noticed several in our dining room area, and as fast as we tipped them out the window more were appearing. We began to suspect that there was a nest close by.

The loft area above the kitchen end had a storage area behind a small trap door. Cautiously opening the entrance, we shone a light to inspect the area. In the corner, on a defunct chimney stack, we saw the most enormous wasp's nest, light grey in colour with several wasps crawling over it. Immediately we shut the door. We were a bit alarmed by the size of this nest, never having seen anything like it before.

Ray emailed our local Mairie with a picture; perhaps they had some suggestions for removing it. A day later a neighbour from the village turned up with our photograph blown up into a large picture. Speaking French, he wanted to establish with us whether it was a hornets' nest as they are the same colour. We assured him it was definitely wasps. He seemed relieved, as apparently we would have needed professional help to destroy a hornet's nest. Expressing his surprise at the size, he explained the best plan was to purchase a special can of killer spray for *guêpes* (wasps) and thoroughly soak the nest.

We put this off for a further few days, but the intrusion of wasps was worrying. Being the smaller, I was elected to be the one to enter through the small doorway, measuring only half a metre high by the same amount in width. Thoroughly covered and masked up against the fumes I summoned up my courage. We opened the entrance again, Ray shining the torch. Nothing had changed, just a few wasps were crawling over it. I aimed the can and pressing hard on the jet button, I sprayed the liquid directly at the nest three feet away. I counted ten seconds, stopped and repeated the action. By now all the contents had been emptied and the nest was truly soaked. The wasps started to fall off the outside of the nest. Quickly the entrance was sealed.

The next day we opened up the hatch and listened. We could hear a slight buzz. Off we went for more cans. Luckily the next spray we purchased gave instructions that it might take a few hours for all the wasps to die. Knowing our nest was enormous, it probably was going to take a day to penetrate. So I repeated the procedure.

We left the nest for a week and no wasps were appearing downstairs. Then we noticed an awful smell, like that of a dead mouse decomposing. The nest had to be removed. A sheet was spread around the nest and I crawled in, trying to ignore the disgusting smell, and with a rake head tool began to pull it away from the wall. The front came away and revealed nine layers similar to cones inside a bee hive. Each layer consisted of hundreds of small cocoon holes where the wasps had grown. Several dozen dead wasps fell out onto the sheet. I continued hacking away until it was all removed and rolled up the sheet taking it outside to dispose of on our acre. Ray vacuumed out the loft area and sprayed it with air-freshener. To build a nest that size must have taken several months. In future we will keep an eye on these hidden areas.

Jack received help to demolish our outbuildings from another ex-pat from England. Like Jack he had left England in his mid-fifties to work for himself in France. We had to admire their determination. Not speaking the language, they had been on a very fast learning curve, applying themselves to the strict codes of work practice and observing all necessary rules and regulations to complete all the paperwork involved in France. They confessed that their annual tax returns had to be undertaken by a local lady translator ensuring legal compliance filling in the forms. It was hard enough to converse with the other tradesmen who they worked alongside, let alone order their materials at the various depots and wood-yards. We knew ourselves how difficult it had been to purchase numerous plumbing and electrical materials. But they were both very happy with their new lives in France and had no regrets at all, only praise for the kindness and help received from the French people. This was conveyed to us as we sat outside joining them at coffee and lunch breaks, enjoying the spring sunshine.

Once the old buildings were removed and the stone debris had been carted away by trailer to the local déchetterie, Jack continued to work on his own. The old very heavy supporting beams were stored in the barn. These beams would be recycled by us and cut down into supports to make the future boat-port. This would be easily accomplished by using Ray's Triton Workmaster, which had already been invaluable in the restoration to date.

When the protective shuttering was taken off the doors the benefit was amazingly apparent. With the outbuildings removed the view of the garden, including our acre of land down to the walnut trees, could be enjoyed from inside the house. A backdrop was provided by the surrounding farmers' fields, with to the right a small forest and to our left the white winding lane - enchanting.

Jack now began work on the 10-centimetre-square green oak beams which would form the outline of the new abri, having previously shown us pictures of ones he had constructed. Because he could get good fixings on the rear of the cottage, over the new doorway, the abri could be kept high. This allowed maximum light into our room.

The weather continued dry and each day was becoming warmer as the weeks went by. By mid-May the abri was complete; Jack had constructed two high steps to enable entry to the lounge. There had been some concrete base left from the outbuildings but the whole area had to be levelled and a sound base constructed to enable the patio area to be laid.

Ray set about laying the base; Jack had marked out the levels for us. He offered to come back to help us do the final screed on which to lay patio tiles. This was planned for the end of May. First we had to complete a level concrete area of approximately four metres square ourselves. This was carried out during the next two weeks.

Jack duly arrived with two tonnes of sand and ten bags of concrete. We operated our concrete mixer, keeping him supplied with the necessary wheelbarrows full of screed mix. The temperature was twenty-nine degrees in the shade, the hottest day of the year so far. Temporary shading was rigged up to stop the screed drying out too fast where the sun shone in the side of the abri. Jack had laid the final mix by 3 pm. We barely found the strength to clean our mixer; exhausted, we collapsed into chairs with ice cold drinks.

The annual visit by Aunty had been arranged for mid-September because the downstairs bedroom was being used as a storage area in the spring. Now having completed the last vital part of the jigsaw, the rooms in the cottage were correct. Also in early October our relatives were flying from Australia to Paris, from where they would fast-train it to us.

We now had to think about returning to England and leaving the cottage ready for our son and his friends. Although the screed was drying out nicely on the patio area, felt it would be better to lay the new ceramic tiles on our return.

We visited the second-hand furniture shop near Périgueux and purchased a solid wood three-metre-long refectory table for the abri. It was very realistically priced and after looking at the new modern teak tables in the garden centres we thought this one suited the area much better. It could easily seat eight to ten people. We knew our son and friends would make full use of this as during their vacation, they virtually lived outside. The abri, facing east, was well situated for morning sunshine, while being open to the south for the afternoon sun.

Finding out that the local village was having its annual *brocante* (car boot sale) that Sunday, I phoned Judy and Brian to come over for a meal under the new abri.

"Come over and we will christen the new extension with lunch and a bottle of plonk" I said. "I know you love visiting a French *vide grenier* [empty your loft], there's one on near us, and we can go before lunch."

So the arrangements were made. We woke to a glorious sunny morning as the forecast had predicted. Lunch could definitely be outside. Saturday had been spent preparing the food as I had planned shell-fish vol-au-vent starters, following by cold chicken salad with various pâtés and cheeses with French pâtisseries to follow.

They arrived early for coffee and agreed our abri had turned out a fabulous success, greatly extending our living space into an outside covered area. "I can't believe the difference this will make for you" said Judy.

A couple of hours were spent enjoying the various stalls. There were about fifty stall-holders with everything you would expect to find turned out of a loft, along with a few specialist stalls of collectors' items who make a habit of attending these sales. Nearly every week during the months from spring to autumn you can find one going on somewhere around the area, as they are very popular with the French.

We returned to celebrate in style and enjoy a lazy afternoon spent catching up with all our news. Two days later we would be returning to England and they would stay to enjoy their cottage in the coming months with summer visitors.

We returned to England jubilant with our efforts in the spring. Our work had changed the cottage so much. We had eaten our evening meal outside during the last few days of our stay. It had been so easy to transport everything from the kitchen to the new table and then enjoy the warmth and smells of the evening as the sun gradually dropped lower in the sky to the front of the cottage, while we sat with the views and sounds of the countryside all around us.

Indeed our son was more than impressed with the new abri and they told us it had put a completely different feel to the property. Paul and Sally take their two Bernese Mountain dogs over to France and have all the rigmarole of sorting out dog passports and injections to comply with the strict rules taking pets abroad. I am assured the dogs enjoy their time there as much as the owners. They are taken out early morning for exercise before it is too hot on the Grand Tour and other walks.

One morning during this year's holiday, Bentley, the younger of the two dogs, was sniffing out the hedgerows when suddenly he was yelping in pain. All of a sudden swarms of bees appeared around Paul and the two children. Bentley had disturbed a wild hive and the bees were on the defensive.

Paul and the kids took to their heels, flapping arms to ward off the pursuing bees. Two dogs bringing up the rear barking at the offending attack. Although stung on his ear, loads of dead bees had suffocated in his fur and had to be removed. Sally carefully disposed of these and administered comfort. Enya, the second dog, although not stung on this occasion, has also been caught out by insects. On her next visit she stepped on a hornet, which gave her a really nasty sting; she sat for days with a paw raised for sympathy.

We returned in early September to prepare the house for visits from various relatives. While visiting Périgueux to look for ceramic patio tiles, we came across a large exhibition, held annually. Staged over several fields, it displayed swimming pools, sheds, garages, tractors and gardening equipment. Several very large marquees contained furniture, kitchens and bedrooms, along with all the usual stands you get at these functions. We were interested to find a company that would erect a wooden garage. Of the several exhibiting garage companies we compared size and finish, choosing one that we thought ideal for us. The son of the owner spoke English. We arranged with him to visit our cottage during the next two weeks to discuss what would be involved.

Meanwhile we commenced the last stage of painting, the rear of the cottage, with the stone paint. The area under the abri was brightened up, matching it into the other sides of the property.

It all started with a written invitation in our mail box. The hameau was organising 'une celebration des voisins' (neighbours' celebration). In our region there was a theme to encourage the French to mix with their English neighbours. From the description in the letter it was going to be more like a street party; friends were also invited. It invited you to make contact with one of the two lady organisers to specify if you would like to bring along an entrée course or a dessert. The date of the event coincided with Aunt Margie's visit, so we hoped she would be happy to join in the spirit of 'vive la France'. The actual event was on the day of her arrival. Luckily it did not begin until 7.30 pm.

That day Aunty had been up since 5 am to catch an 8 am flight from East Midlands airport. When we met our visitor at Bergerac Airport we thought it best not to impart the news about the forthcoming late night until she had had time to settle in.

Weatherwise it was a beautiful day, warming up into a hot afternoon. The village had been decorated with various streamers on posts and gates; one long table had been assembled in the farmer's courtyard, this being the chosen venue. Aunty was more than keen to come along, and being a very young eighty-two she set off with us at 7.30 pm. Between us we were laden with three large individual plates of desserts and two bottles of rosé. The usual format of apéritifs ensued; two trestle tables had been laid up with drinks and hors-d'oeuvres. Although there was just about every choice of drink, including two litre bottles of whisky, we stuck to our preferred pineau. Not just any pineau, this was home-made by the farmer's wife, and although delicious it contained far more brandy than the normal recipe.

We recognised most of our neighbours and introduced Aunty to them, and meanwhile villagers' friends were arriving by the minute. Every person who arrived shook hands with all those present and the obligatory three kisses were administered to all the females. Even young children were expected to say their "bonsoirs" and offer their faces for kisses. The apéritifs lasted until 9 pm and then, at last, it seemed as though the meal was going to commence.

We counted forty-two places laid up at the long table, so as there were only twelve homes in the village, a lot of the guests had to be friends and relatives. We were the only English people attending; luckily, I managed to get us seated by Marie-Odette and her friends, which would help with the conversation as she understood my limited French.

The older men seated themselves at the far end of the table where, no doubt, they could enjoy their reminiscing. Then the rest of the guests took their places and the entrées were passed along the table. The ladies organising the event were spreading the baskets of bread and bottles of water at intervals along the table and several of the men were distributing a choice of wines. The feast was beginning. The main course was very tender thick slices of pork, cooked in the farmer's kitchen and not spit roasted. Accompanying the pork were dishes of vegetables and more crusty bread, along with plenty of wine.

Luckily the weather had stayed good; as darkness was beginning to fall the evening was still quite warm, although you needed a jumper on your shoulders. The next course followed - plates of cheese with grapes and celery. As on previous events we had attended, the better wine was now appearing. Numerous bottles of cru Pomerol had been provided by the gentleman who lived in the large manor-type property opposite the lake. Finally les desserts, which had been laid out on the tables formerly used for the apéritifs; we could help ourselves from the selection on offer.

It was soon 11.30 pm, and it was amazing how Aunty had managed to keep going. Ray and I felt tired from all the day's activity and trying our best to keep up with the French conversation. We thanked the organisers and said our "au revoirs" before joining our neighbour, Marie-Odette, who had remembered to bring a torch. We linked arms and made our way back through the village in the pitch dark. No doubt the remaining guests would continue chatting until the early hours, but for us it was time to 'hit the sack'.

Next morning we were up fairly early, including Aunty; we had all paced ourselves quite carefully on the wine, having learned lessons from previous occasions when so much alcohol was on offer. The reason for the early start was that it was Sunday and there was a special event taking place in a 'beaux village' the other side of Périgueux.

During the following week we enjoyed a lovely day at Brantôme, a small town surrounded by water a few miles outside Périgueux. They call it 'Little Venice'. We walked around the abbey, which is idyllically sited on the river. After lunch we took the boat trip which cruised around the waterways. It was a great way to see the historical buildings, passing so close from the river, especially the abbey, which fronts onto the water. Luckily it was not too crowded as this village attracts a lot of tourists.

Another very interesting event that month, which unfortunately did not coincide with our visitor's dates, was 'Ouvert des Portes', or Open Day. The village of St Privat-des-Prés where we have our Mairie for all matters of importance, including collecting *sacs jaune* (yellow sacks) for the recycling rubbish, has its own Musée de Vie (Museum of Life.) It is open in the summer for tourists and organised by volunteers. This special open day was not only opening up the Musée; it was going to use local people of the village to dress in the clothes of everyday people in times past and demonstrate the ancient implements from the museum which depicted rural French life across the last two centuries.

Among the many demonstrations of medieval-looking instruments the one thing I remember was how they made wooden shoes. These are called *sabots* or clogs and were worn in our area well into the early 20th century. Several of the presenters in costume were actually wearing sabots. After the outside demonstrations there followed an interesting tour around the Musée itself. We saw relics of all kinds, donated from past and present village inhabitants. Many photographs of life as it was reminded us how lucky we are now with our modern services. Water was hand-pumped up from wells, and an electric pump was not fitted until the 1950s. Up to then there had been no electricity in the village.

Lastly there was a demonstration at the *lavoir*, the public washing area, now a tourist attraction in many French towns. We watched as the ladies in period costume acted out how they would meet and wash their sheets in the running water. As usual the event finished with drinks and nibbles which were laid on at a new art classroom which had been recently opened, with interesting pictures from local artists depicting past village life.

As previously arranged, the owner of the garage company, along with his son Damien, arrived to take all the measurements. He was happy to sit lazily under the abri, drinking a Pineau and discussing pleasantries of the day, along with the best area to site our garage. There was no urgency about his visit and he was able to answer all concerns over the project. He wrote out the devis which formed the final quotation and against which we paid the customary deposit. A provisional date was given to commence the concrete base.

Although the size of the garage was within permitted limits to be classed as portable, it would be considered prudent to advise our local Mairie. It was to be quite a distance away from the house near the driveway entrance but, as advised, two metres in from our boundary. Luckily it would be obscured from view by a very wide fifteen-foot-high laurel shrub.

Preferring not to leave ourselves open to any repercussions from neighbours, we visited the Mairie. Although we took all the necessary documents provided by the garage owner, needless to say, we still had to complete forms to be forwarded to Périgueux for planning permission. We were told it could take up to seven weeks, depending on when the council next sat. Unable to wait that length of time for confirmation we decided to press on with construction and keep our fingers crossed.

After Aunty's departure we had two weeks before the arrival of our Australian visitors. A new goal - we needed to lay the patio tiles before their visit. The weather then suddenly turned cold and wet, which delayed us for a couple of days. Fortunately it ensured we spent a while planning the best point to start. This would ensure the tiles would look as though they had been laid professionally. We took extra thought in positioning them up to and around the high steps.

The job was fairly straightforward although a lot of time was spent cutting the tiles for the steps and edging. The last stage was removing the spacers and grouting between the tiles. It certainly improved the area, making it easy to sweep and keep clean. We proudly returned the large table on the light coloured beige tiles.

Damien telephoned to say he could now come and lay our concrete base. This was to be completed in one day, an unbelievable amount of work considering that Damien and his young helper turned up at around 9 am, unloaded their concrete mixer and worked with materials from the back of their open lorry. We had already removed the turf from an area approximately six metres by three metres, leaving it roughly levelled with exposed earth.

Using shuttering they outlined the levels of the base; the slope of the ground meant the base would be built up a good thirty centimetres at the rear, reducing to fifteen centimetres at the front. It was critical that the base was square, as the intended garage was in pre-formed sections and required to fit exactly.

We supplied them with drinks and encouragement, but by 5 pm they had used up all the sand and had about an eighth left to complete. Deciding it was too late to go to Ribérac to purchase extra sand, they decided to return the next day. Clearly they would have preferred to finish the job, as they were based in a town near Bergerac, about one and half hour's journey away.

An hour later we were sitting inside the house having our evening meal when we heard water running. Knowing it was not the washing machine or any other appliance, we realised it was coming from the outside water tap. Damien and his partner had returned and were both busy mixing concrete. Apparently Damien had stopped for fuel at the St Aulaye garage and met the owner of the local company from whom we had purchased our stones for the front of the house. This man knew Damien's father and his garage company, so he was prepared to let Damien have enough sand to complete the job from his local depot. So at 7.30 the work continued. They finally finished at 9.30 with darkness falling. We now had to let the base dry for a good four weeks before the garage was delivered and erected.

We collected Ann and Ian from Angoulême after their journey from Paris on the TGV, having flown from Adelaide three days before. Recognition of all our efforts over the last three years was expressed, enthusing about the new doorway to the garden. On their initial visit, three years ago, the new rooms upstairs were barely outlined with partitions. They genuinely praised our small cottage, its rural situation and its value as a base from which to explore France. "Too right mate, it's a little gem!" said Ian in his broad Australian accent.

We felt quite flattered that they had wanted to return to our cottage to see our improvements, considering all the attractions they were going to see after visiting us. Their planned route was by luxury train from Bordeaux, stopping at Montpellier, Marseilles, Cannes, and Nice. Leaving France they would cross into Italy by train to Milan, Florence and Rome.

Sitting in a local restaurant in the next village, we study the menu, which offers an immense variety of pizza freshly-cooked by the Italian chef.

"Nous voulons partager une pizza, s'il vous plaît" (we wish to share a pizza) I say to the waitress. I point to Ann and Ian opposite, who have chosen the same pizza, indicating they too wanted to share a pizza, saying "encore la même" (same again). The French take you literally. We were served one pizza divided into four. We all laughed and requested "une autre pizza, svp!"

It's like that with the French; it just has to be exactly as you have said, no give or take. Their language is so exacting. That's why you have to sound every syllable and pitch it just right to be understood. Ray has often said "je voudrais du beurre" (I want some butter) but his pronunciation has been more like "deux bières" and more than once we have had two glasses of beer brought to the table. We just say "désolé". It always sorts itself out.

For the next week we lived outside, sitting at the new table over long discussions and lazy lunches. At the end of their short stay the plan was to take them to Chalais station for a train to Bordeaux, where they would start their European tour. Two days before their departure when we arrived at Chalais to purchase a ticket to Bordeaux, the notice at the ticket desk said "un grève situation". A railway strike was planned on the first day of their trip. With reservations in Bordeaux for their pre-planned holiday, a decision was made to take them to Bordeaux ourselves. We would park at the newly-constructed park and ride, catching a new tram into the city centre.

All went to plan; we enjoyed a lovely day walking along the waterfront and travelling by the new trams to various parts of the city. We took them to the old quarter of St Michael and showed them the large antique halls, then had lunch outside in a café opposite the waterfront. They were booked into a hotel for two nights so they could continue with more sight-seeing the following day, before the first leg of their planned train holiday.

Luckily for them no full-day train strikes were planned during the rest of their stay in the cities of France along the Mediterranean. It could have been a problem, as their tickets were already purchased with tight schedules for the route.

Returning to our cottage and sitting in the warm evening air, the smell of the barbecue lingering, we sat silent. Having enjoying thick lamb chops and salad along with all the trimmings, we drank the remains of the Bordeaux rouge. The sky was taking on the red glow of sunset, promising another warm settled day tomorrow. We were pleased our relations had been able to witness all the improvements. Now it was nice just to enjoy the silence of the evening. No more tales of Australian life ad-libs of "young floozies", feeling "crook" and getting rid of the "shrapnel" (loose change). Australians do have a lot of quirky language. Although, on reflection, Ian's comment about our cottage being "a little gem" certainly hit the spot. With the improvements almost finished we could now think of it as precious.

Wondering what the French is for little gem I consulted my dictionary; it showed "petit joyau". The little jewel. Ray decided he would make the necessary name plate to fix on the outside front wall, so at long last our cottage had earned its rightful name in our hamlet.

We enjoy our visitors and showing off our local places of interest. We are quite surprised that our visitors always want to return, especially as it is a small cottage and far from a grand French maison. But the situation is very peaceful, and with views of the countryside you can't help but feel in touch with nature.

Our son and his friends keep returning each year because, as they tell us, "We just chill out, eat the most wonderful French food, drink fantastic wine and totally relax." I'm sure they would agree "it's a little gem".

We should not guard our tranquillity so jealously – but we do. Tonight we are visited by the redstarts; great tits take a quick bath in the bird bath and jays fly past us, followed by a flock of magpies making for the tall poplar trees and calling out with their high-pitched screeching. Blackbirds seeking the last meal of the day stop by us for a few moments and then take flight again. As dusk begins to fall the temperature drops a couple of degrees, but it is still showing twenty-three degrees on the gauge. The moon is rising in the distance; tonight will be a full moon, according to the diary.

We feel a further drop in the air temperature; time to return inside. Plans are made for tomorrow, the weekly trip to Ribérac, and the list is prepared.

After the Australian's departure we had three weeks left before our return to England. We had intended to complete the walk-in wardrobe, not having had the time back in the spring, but having decided to enlarge the project, incorporating cupboard spaces either end with an upper shelf for storage, we would now leave it to our return next spring.

Instead we planned to enjoy a short holiday. We had always intended to visit the town of Carcassonne in the foothills of the Pyrenees. Just outside the main town there was a fortified medieval town known as "La Cité", the largest walled city in Europe.

A few years earlier we had been travelling around this area exploring the possibilities of buying a property. Travelling along the A61-E80 motorway I happened to look over to the right and the sunlight highlighted the most beautiful coloured fortress walls, soft beige, sand and yellows to soft mauves and brown. It really takes your breath away when you see the outline of Carcassonne. Towers and turrets break the skyline and you know it's so amazing that you want to explore further.

Reading up about this area, we felt sure it would be a fascinating place for a trip. Searching our hotel book, *Châteaux and Hotels of France*, I found a perfect venue about five kilometres from La Cité. It was the Château de Cavanac, advertising beautifully-restored rooms set in twenty acres of their own *vignoble* (vineyard). They had vacancies as it was later in the season.

Following a map offered at the hotel, we easily found La Cité with its large designated parking areas, for a small daily charge. From there you could walk through the imposing gateway into the walls of the city. We were fully expecting to pay an admission charge into such an historical and fascinating place, but entry was free. Like so many attractions in France, you are always surprised at the fairness of the price. Unlike England, where there is always an exorbitant cost totally out of proportion to the number of people wishing to visit historical places.

Once through the outer fortress walls, there was a circuit of ramparts between another set of fortress walls completely encircling the city. It is a double-walled city. Entry is along a double drawbridge over a large, deep, dry moat into the inner walls. The city's inhabitants live in an assortment of houses contained within the walls. Among the inner buildings along the narrow roads are many tourist shops, cafés and restaurants. We made our way through the avenues towards the spire of the cathedral.

History tells that in 1096 a Romanesque nave was begun, completed during the 12th century. The cathedral was completed over the 13th and 14th centuries. St-Nazaire and Celse Basilica, as it is known, contains tombs of bishops and noble men. Parts were destroyed during 1793 during the Revolution, but modern-day work has continued in renovating it.

At the time of our visit scaffolding was around the building as repairs to the roof were under way. Likewise restoration of the city itself continues daily. It is constantly monitored for improvements; something of this size would seem a never-ending challenge, being of such of such historical value to France. Contained within the walls, as one would expect, is the original Comtal Castle, which is open for guided tours of various durations including an exhibition of fifteenth century costumes and the Lapidary museum.

We spent a fascinating day walking the circuits, as well as enjoying all the everyday life amongst the streets and stopping for our lunch in an open square along with the other tourists. The day culminated with a "visite en calèche" (horse-drawn carriage) which took us around the Circuit *entre les 2 remparts* with a commentary in English. This described the history of battles within the walls of this most famous and intriguing monument.

We returned to the Château de Cavanac for our second evening. Wisely we had pre-booked into the restaurant, which was in the former stables and decorated to present an old-style atmosphere. Suspended on the walls were the large yoke harnesses of the old workhorses, accompanied by a museum-like collection of original farming implements, all interspersed with torch lanterns. The low heavily-beamed ceiling and flagon floor added up to a banqueting room with the atmosphere of a castle.

By 8 pm the restaurant was gradually filling with customers, not necessarily people from the hotel as they only had a half a dozen de luxe bedrooms and a few luxurious four-poster bedrooms. This cuisine was about to be enjoyed by people from the local area. Along the left-hand side was the most enormous covered counter, laid out with meat and fish for your choice. After selection it was traditionally cooked over a wood fire which was already glowing.

The tables were laid up with wine glasses gleaming by candlelight and table lamps. Bottles of wine were placed on the tables from their own vineyards, rouge, blanc and rosé. You only paid for what you consumed, and if you only had a half a bottle that's all you were charged for.

The menu was extensive; the atmosphere from people

totally engrossed in enjoying their evening was amazing. Families and friends were being indulged by a waitressing service with the attention to detail that the French expect. Deep discussions ensued between customer and waiter, ensuring each understood exactly what the menu entailed and knew the cooking time. We yielded to our surroundings and enjoyed the courtesy of the whole evening.

Returning to the main château building, we luxuriated in the opulence of our spacious room; antique furniture, sumptuous curtains and covers, an enormous double en suite bathroom, all for the price you would pay for a modest double room in a city in England.

The following morning, after *petit déjeuner*, we purchased a dozen bottles of their château-labelled wine before setting off on our return journey. As always in France you felt privileged for being allowed to enjoy their special home and hospitality.

During the last week Damien returned to complete erection of the new sectional garage. As before, they hoped to complete the installation the same day. The structure was unloaded and each piece was individually positioned, the sides being formed of thin wooden strips reinforced with metal edging and tied into together with strong bolts and nuts. The roof was time-consuming to construct. It was composed of individual tiles laid over a supporting base. With the strong winds of the Dordogne, the garage sides had to be cemented inside to the new base. Lastly, the two large doors were eased into the front access, ensuring a good fit with inside bolts and an outside lock. As on their previous visit, darkness was falling and we assisted them in rigging up temporary lights so they could continue. It was almost 10 pm when we helped them load up their lorry with the remains of shuttering and the tools and equipment.

We were very grateful to them for getting the garage completed before our departure. The following morning, in daylight, we could inspect the finished building. It fulfilled all our expectations. The car was tried for size, and it allowed more than adequate space to house our ladders, cement mixer, mowers and bikes. It was comforting to know that on our departure the car would be securely locked away.

So we were nearing the end of stay; we had the customary chores regarding the walnut harvest, knuckling the front trees, cutting shrubs and burning the rubbish. We said our farewells to the neighbours as we did an evening walk through the village.

Finally the annual *fermeture de la maison*; all bedding was covered in plastic and stored away against damp, fridges emptied and cleaned. Kitchen cupboards were cleared and only full jars of provisions left ready for our return.

On our last evening we take a trip to a new small restaurant at a local village to enjoy a simple farewell meal. We order an apéritif of Pineau and a pichet of the local wine to accompany the meal. This year we feel we can truly toast ourselves - the 'petite maison' project is complete, after all the travelling to and from France, pulling the indispensable trailer, loaded to the brim with building materials and high hopes to achieve our goal. Each visit has been a new venture.

The hard work has been taken in our stride, and enjoyed rather than endured.

When embarking on our project we could not possibly have envisaged how much we would gain: new friends, helpful and friendly neighbours and continual enjoyment of the rural countryside.

And yet, like any true DIY person, we will always find plenty more jobs. Already planned are a boat-port (timber already provided, thanks to the old beams); repairs to the front wall; a new tiled roof over the front porch; removal of the forty feet of privet hedge and replacement with new fencing (to saving cutting twice a year); a new window in the side of the workshop to let in daylight... and so on, and so on. It is a never-ending adventure.

Epilogue

Now our story has been told; the neglected cottage has finally been restored and enlarged. You entered our cottage on a chilly morning in February and now you are departing in late October. There is a frost on the lawn, the sun is beaming its early rays onto the abri as it burns off the light mist hanging in the morning air. Distant sounds of bugles, shouts and shots come from the *chasseurs* deep in the surrounding forests.

The trees now provide a different backdrop to the countryside with their vivid autumn colours, signalling the anticipation of winter. The farmers have successfully gathered their summer harvests, with only a few crops still standing. Already we see the gently undulating fields being turned over by harrows coupled to small tractors. The dark, finely-tilled earth containing the seeds for next year's growth steams in the sun. The sparrow hawk sits on his usual spot along the telephone line; he explodes into flight as our taxi sweeps by, our destination the airport.

We, like the migrating birds, are departing to a different

country, though unlike the birds, we are already planning our next return trip. Memories of our days at the cottage and the years of happiness spent there remain strong. It has become not just a building but a new way of life; a freedom and a forceful purpose to which we return, enabling us to enjoy the special lifestyle that France has to offer.

ND - #0437 - 270225 - C14 - 203/127/25 - PB - 9781861511546 - Matt Lamination